Harriet Louise Jerome, Stella W. Carroll

Boys and Girls of the Philippines and around the World

Harriet Louise Jerome, Stella W. Carroll

Boys and Girls of the Philippines and around the World

ISBN/EAN: 9783337193942

Printed in Europe, USA, Canada, Australia, Japan

Cover: Foto ©ninafisch / pixelio.de

More available books at **www.hansebooks.com**

OF THE

PHILIPPINES

AND

AROUND THE WORLD

BY

STELLA W. CARROLL AND HARRIET L. JEROME

THE MORSE COMPANY
NEW YORK   BOSTON
1899

ALASKA.

MEXICO.

NORWAY.

SWEDEN.

CUBA.

PORTO RICO.

PHILIPPINES.

HAWAII.

STATUE OF WILLIAM TELL.

AROUND THE WORLD.

ALASKA.

AN ALASKAN HOUSE.

Tipoochac lives in this house. Do you see him standing beside his father with the dogs on the door-step? Is there a brick chimney on their house like the one on your house?

No, there is only a smoke-hole in the middle of the roof, with boards standing up around it. Tipoochac's father is very tired, because he has been on a long journey, carrying heavy tools over the mountains for white men.

Why have so many white men gone to Alaska? What

TIPOOCHAC'S FATHER AND MOTHER.

place beyond Alaska are they trying to reach, and would you like to go there?

Tipoochac's name means "a white fish." There are people in Alaska from almost every country, but the native people of Alaska are all either Indians or Eskimos. What does "native" mean?

Tipoochac's father and mother are Indians, but do not live in tents like the Indians in the other parts of our country. They do not ride fast ponies as some Indians do, but they go about in canoes, for their homes are always near the water. They build large, strong houses and two or three families live in each house.

Here are Tipoochac's father and mother. See the queer, long ear-rings his father has in his ears. Each ring has a seal's tooth hanging from it to bring luck.

The blanket he is wearing cost a dollar and a half. If you should ask him how much his ear-rings are worth, he would say, "Four blankets." That means four times a dollar and a half.

He will tell you the price of everything in blankets. His wife's cape is made of a better red and yellow blanket. She will say that her cape cost two blankets. That means two blankets worth a dollar and a half each. For the silk handkerchiefs they are wearing they paid half a blanket's worth of fish. How much would that be in our money?

Tipoochac and his brother and their father bathe in the sea every day. How would you like a bath in the cold sea water in the winter?

After they come out of the ocean they sometimes have to beat each other with twigs to get warm again. It makes them very strong to bathe in the cold salt water. Their mother tells them that it will help them to be brave chiefs when they are men. Tipoochac would like to be a great chief. Come with Tipoochac and he will show you his grandfather's home. You must be ready to climb into the house, for the door is small and high. But who is sick? It is his grandfather, and he has been ill a long time. And you ask me if he has had a doctor? Yes, the doctor is here now with the sick man.

Perhaps you have never seen a doctor dressed just as

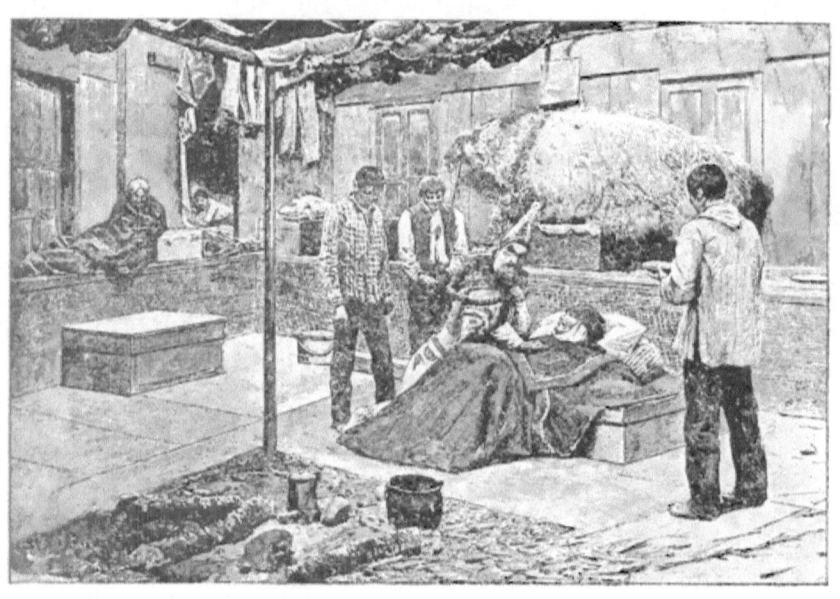

TIPOOCHAC'S GRANDFATHER AND THE DOCTOR.

this one is. He is a sorcerer; if you do not know what that long word means, ask some one to tell you. He gives Tipoochac's grandfather no medicine, but tells him he will soon be well.

Is this the only room in this house? Yes; one part of it is used for bedrooms, another part for a pantry, and an other for a kitchen. In the middle of the room there are no boards on the ground. This bare ground is covered with stones, and is used as a fireplace. Tipoochac's grandmother cooks here. She mixes flour and water and makes cakes. She fries the cakes in salmon oil.

Tipoochac brings her the oil in a horn spoon. He gets it from the carved chest which his grandfather made.

Every dish is made of wood, and is handsomely carved.

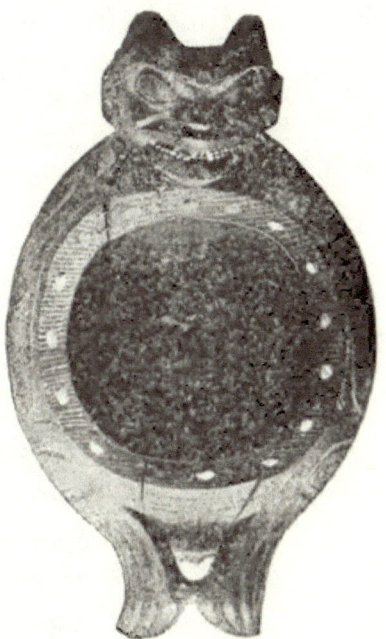

A DISH.

The spoons are made from the horns of mountain goats. They are carved or painted. Would you like to use one of their long queer berry spoons? They eat huckleberries, and gooseberries, and cranberries, and salmonberries, and strawberries, with them. This dish is made of wood and has shells inlaid or set into the edge.

A DISH.

Do you think Tipoochac's grandmother can cook anything over the fire in wooden dishes? No, the fire would

14   AROUND THE WORLD.

burn the dishes. She heats stones very hot, then she drops them into the soup that she wishes to cook, and that makes the soup boil. The dish is as large as a washbowl and is very heavy. The spoon is made of a goat's horn, and has a long carved handle. The handles of some dishes are carved to look like men's heads.

Do you have such odd dishes at your home, and does your father carve out of wood the dishes that you use?

Tipoochac is still a little boy, but he has learned to carve. He would like a sharp knife like yours. His father made him a knife with a flint blade, with two eagles carved one above the other on the wooden handle. The blade is tied to the handle with a cord made of the roots of a spruce tree, split and twisted.

Tipoochac can carve a dish out of a block of wood. Where will he find the wood? He can chop down a tree himself. Long ago, before the Alaskans could trade with white men, they made their own axes.

How would you make an ax if you were away off in the woods? Here is a picture of an ax that the Alaskans made. The handle is

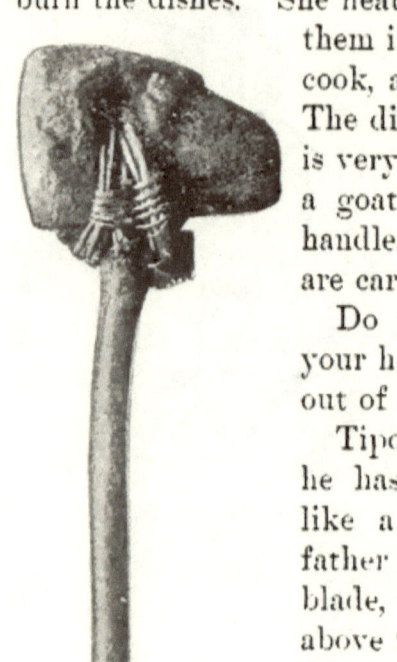

AN AX.

a strong piece of hard wood. How do you think they made it smooth? They used a rough piece of shark's skin for sand-paper.

The head of the ax is a piece of flint. What is the hardest kind of stone, and where is it found? The flint is sharpened on each edge and hollowed across the sides by chipping it with another piece of flint. Do you think it would be easy to sharpen a stone in this way?

The head of the ax is tied to the handle with a strong cord. The cord is made of spruce roots which have been split and twisted together. Could you chop down a tree with this ax? If you made an ax of stone and wood how would you fasten the head to the handle?

Here comes a chief dressed in his fine clothes. You could not buy them for hundreds of dollars. He is going

AN ALASKAN CHIEF.

16 AROUND THE WORLD.

CHIEF'S CROWN.

to a feast and has on his best suit, which is trimmed with furs and shells, and the beaks of many birds.

See the rattle or clapper made of wood, that he has in his hand. The chief will shake it when he dances at the great feast. Why is the rattle carved in this way?

The chief is very proud of the copper ring he has in his nose. The crown on his head is made of wood, and must be heavy. The carvings on the crown tell what a great man he is and to which party or totem he belongs.

Walrus whiskers stand up around the top of his crown, and inside of this little fence of whiskers there is eider down. The down will fall out and look like a snowstorm when the chief dances. Ermine skins are hung from the back of his crown. Do you know how much ermine fur costs?

The chief's coat is made of cloth which his grandmother wove long ago. The threads which run up and down are made of cedar bark. The bark

CHIEF'S COAT.

is scraped from a tree and soaked in water many days and then it is beaten into fibers with a mallet made from the bone of a deer.

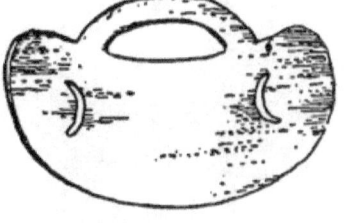

An Indian woman twists these fibers into a fine thread by rubbing them between her hands. The threads which go across are made from the wool of goats. The wool is colored yellow and black and brown.

A MALLET.

The threads are woven in and out very much as we weave patterns in the kindergarten. The figures on the chief's coat and blanket also

CHIEF'S BLANKET.

show to which totem he belongs. How many faces can you see on his coat? How many pairs of eyes can you see

18   AROUND THE WORLD.

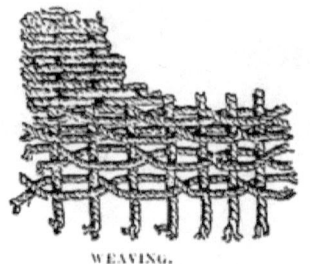      

WEAVING.   LEGGING.

on his blanket? The fringe is also made of the soft silky wool of the goat. How would your father like to wear such a blanket for an overcoat? A blanket like this one is worth forty dollars.

The chief's leggings are made of deerskin, and are trimmed with fringes. Birds' beaks are fastened to these fringes, and when the chief dances the beaks rattle.

The chief lives in this house with his great family.

EXTERIOR OF CHIEF'S HOUSE.

Why are those tall carved poles in front of each house? They are totem poles, and are put up to show who lives in the house. Each Indian must marry a woman who belongs to another totem, so there are always two totems in a family. The children belong to their mother's totem.

This pole is in front of the chief's house. The chief belongs to the bear totem. Do you see the bear at the top

INTERIOR OF CHIEF'S HOUSE.

of the column? The chief's wife and children belong to the beaver totem, so there is a beaver sitting at the bottom of the pole. This pole is placed near the doorway of the house. Would you like to go inside? Here is a picture of what you would see.

The chief would never kill a bear, because he belongs to the bear totem. He thinks all bears are his friends and so

TOTEM POLES.

he is kind to them. His wife tells her children that they must never kill a beaver, for they belong to the beaver totem.

She says all beavers belong to their family. When the chief goes fishing he has pictures of the bear painted on his boat, and the bear's picture is carved on the paddles and wooden fishhooks.

The chief thinks this will please the bear, so that its spirit will help him catch fish. His wife has the beaver painted or carved on everything she uses. Even the paint brushes will have totems carved on their handles.

Above the beaver on the totem pole is a carving of the bear eating the hunter who came to steal the bear's wife. Above that is the Great Raven who stole the new moon and carried it away in his beak.

The Indians think the Great Raven made the first people who lived on the earth. Some day we will read the stories they tell about him.

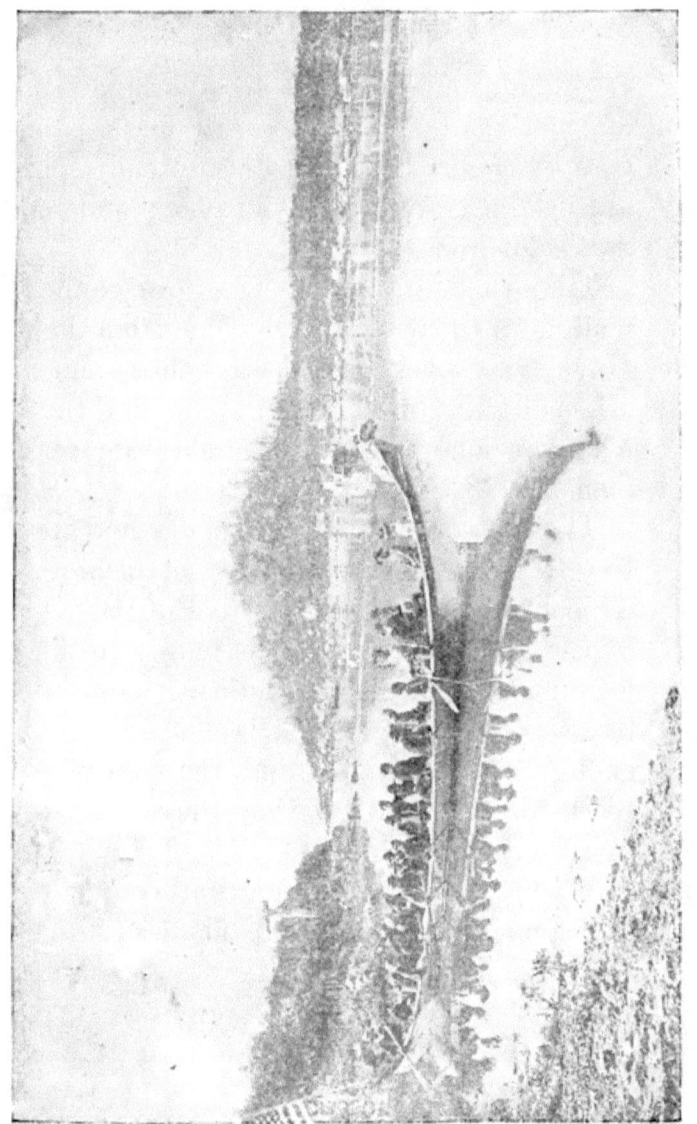

A FAMILY OR WAR CANOE.

When an Indian goes to a strange village he looks at the totem poles until he finds where a man lives who belongs to his totem. This man must take care of the stranger and make a dance for him.

Tipoochac's father owns a large canoe. It is made of a great log which came from the woods. Have you ever been in a canoe, and was it all made in one piece? I do not think you ever saw one that would hold fourteen men.

These are family or war canoes, and are too large to use in hunting or fishing. Tipoochac does not always live in the village. His father takes his family to the fishing grounds or to his hunting lodge to live a part of the year. His canoe is large enough for his family, and the men who work for him, and all that they wish to carry with them.

When Tipoochac's grandfather made the canoe he had only tools made of bone and flint. Would you like to see him make one of these large canoes?

First he finds a fine great cedar tree as large around as a tub and very straight. He cuts it down partly with his ax and partly by burning the trunk near the ground. He watches his fire and does not let it burn the outside of the tree.

TOTEM POLE.

CHISEL.

He fells the tree into the water if he can, so that he can float it home.

When winter comes he will make a canoe out of it. He will cut a log fifteen feet long from the tree and will then raise it from the ground on some sticks. The bark will be peeled off and a slow fire made on top of the log. Tipoochac and his grandfather will watch the fire. He will burn it just where he wishes to hollow out the log. Then he will chip away the charred wood with a horn chisel and a stone mallet.

They will burn the outside until it is of nearly the right shape. Then the charred wood will be chipped away from this side, and Tipoochac will fill the canoe with water. He will then build a fire and heat stones red hot, and his grandfather will drop the red-hot stones into the water until it boils.

The boiling water makes the wood as soft as leather. Then his grandfather will put in poles to stretch the canoe wider and he will make it pointed at the ends.

When it is of the right shape the canoe will be sand-papered with shark skin. It will be dried and oiled with fish oil, and painted. The outside will be black and the inside white. It will have a red stripe painted all around it. Tipoochac's grandfather could make canoes much easier with steel tools, but he thinks it would bring bad luck to the canoe if he used white men's tools.

AN AWL.

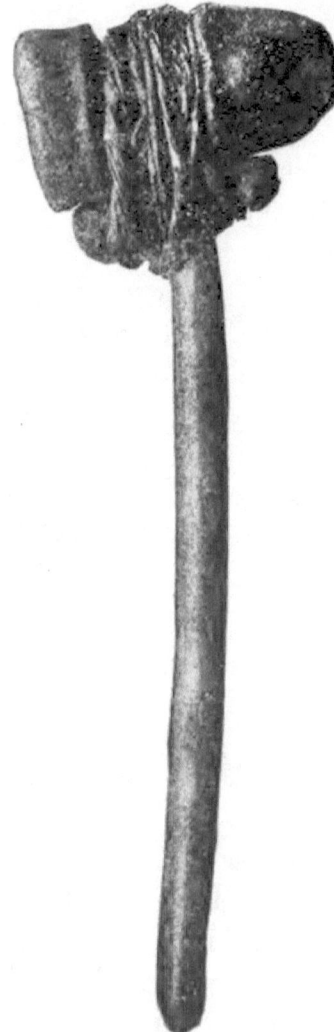

AN AX.

So he makes his own ax and hammer and chisel out of bone and stone. The canoe will be as fine as any in the world. A man can go fifty miles out to sea in this canoe. Some of the finest steamships in New York harbor have been copied from Alaskan canoes.

This Indian lives in another part of Alaska. He wears very little clothing in summer. He spears fish while his wife paddles the canoe. His canoe is made of strips of tough wood covered with deer skins.

This Indian is making a larger canoe. He will sew the skins together, with cords made of cedar bark. First he will make holes with awls made of fish bone; then he will sew the skins together. He will fill the holes that the awl makes, with pitch.

He makes his canoe small and light, so that he can carry it around water-falls on his head.

AN AWL.

ALASKA. 25

ALASKAN INDIAN VILLAGE.

Tipoochac's father has a small canoe. He will take very good care of both of his canoes. He will cover them with blankets when he leaves them on the shore, as you would cover a fine horse on a cold day.

In the hunting season Tipoochac will go with his father to their lodge in the woods. Many deer will be shot with their arrows, and many fish in the bay will be caught. They will kill black bears, for they like the tender bear meat.

HUNTING LODGE.

They are afraid of the great brown bear. If they see his tracks they will shout pleasant things about him. They think this will keep the bear from being angry; what do you think? If the chief was hunting would he kill a bear? Why not?

Here is an Alaskan bow and arrow. Did you ever see a real Indian arrow, and of what was

the arrow-head made? How were all the little feathers on the other end of the arrow put in?

A deer can swim a long distance. Sometimes Tipoochac's father sees a herd of deer coming to drink in the lake. Tipoochac and the dogs drive the deer into the water, and then get on his back and kill him.

KILLING DEER.

When no deer come the men call them with a whistle. The deer whistle makes a little crying noise like a deer calling its mate. They make the whistle by blowing on a blade of grass held between two strips of wood.

Can you whistle on a blade of grass which you hold between your hands? When Tipoochac's grandfather blows on the grass the deer think another deer is calling them. Tipoochac likes deer meat, or venison.

His father will sell the deer skin to the white men, but he will save the horns and bones until next winter. He will make spoons and tools and fish-hooks of them.

Sitka is a queer little city, many miles away. Native Indians live in one part of it, while white men from many countries live in the other part. There is a wall between the two parts of the city.

At nine o'clock every morning a gate in the wall is opened. Indian women and children come through the gate into the white men's part of the town. They bring berries and fish and carvings and bead work to sell.

TOTEM POLES.

When they have sold them the women buy bright calicoes at the stores.

The Indian men are away hunting or fishing many weeks. When they are at home they come into the white men's part of the town. Just before three o'clock a guard goes

INDIAN WOMEN.

through all the crooked little streets and sends the Indians out of the gates. After they have gone out the gate is locked. There is a guard house near the gate. From this guard house officers watch over the Indian part of the town day and night.

Would you like some berries for dinner, and if so, what kind of berries will you have? There are raspberries, and strawberries and currants and huckleberries in the pails.

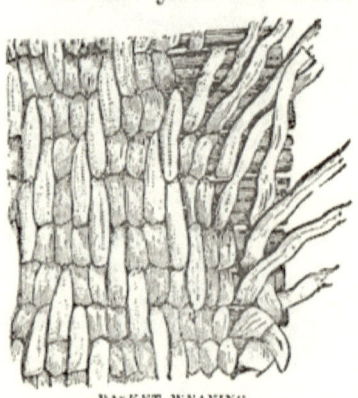

BASKET WEAVING.

One woman has a large box made of bearskin, in which are thimbleberries. Another woman has cranberries in a basket which she made. It is made of spruce roots and grass which

AN ALASKAN TOMB.

are colored yellow and black and brown. This is the way in which it is made.

Some of these baskets will hold water. If the women do not sell all their berries they will take them home and bury them. That will keep them for winter.

INDIAN MYTHS.

Kit-Elswa, a boy who lives in Alaska, made these pictures. This is a picture of a whale killer.

The Alaskans think the whale killer lives in the ocean and has a head like a raven, with many beaks, and a tail like a man's head. They tell the children that he can change his form, but they think that there is always a man living in him.

One day long ago, they say, some boys threw stones at what they thought to be a great black fish. The fish was frightened and swam to the shore. When the boys ran to see it, they

SKANA, THE WHALE KILLER, AS DRAWN BY A YOUNG ALASKAN INDIAN.

found not a fish, but a man in a bark canoe.

The man was cooking some food. "You broke my canoe with stones," he said, "so you must mend it."

The boys took some small roots and mended it. "Now turn your backs to the water and put your blankets over your heads," said the man. The boys did as they were told, and soon the man called, "Now look!" They looked and saw the canoe rising on the first breakers. Then it became the whale killer, with its raven's head and its tail that looked like a man's head.

This raven used to go to the bottom of the sea and steal the bait from the fishermen's hooks. At last a fisherman caught the raven with a magic hook.

The fisherman took the raven ashore, but he turned himself into a man. His wings became a blanket, and he hid his face in it.

At last when he was peeping out a young man threw

something into his eyes. This made him very angry, and he dropped the blanket and flew away. Ever since that time the ravens and the crows have troubled the Indians in every way possible.

One day the moon saw a man dip his bucket into a brook for water. The moon sent down its long rays and drew the man up to the sky.

The man tried to save himself by grasping a bush, but the moon was so strong that it drew up the man, bucket, bush, and all.

He has lived in the moon ever since. Whenever it rains it is because this man is emptying his bucket.

NETS.

Nownak and her sister are catching salmon. They have a long net tied to a pole. Be careful, Nownak, or the salmon will get away. He is large and strong and can swim very fast.

There are many salmon in the river. Nownak's mother has an iron kettle, which she bought of white men, in which she cooks the salmon.

All the oil will rise to the top of the water. When it cools she will save the oil to be used in winter.

She will smoke some of the salmon and dry them for winter. The Eskimos eat the dried fish when it has been dipped in fish oil.

Did you ever taste of fish oil? Nownak likes cod-liver oil and salmon oil and seal oil as well as you like butter. Sometimes she eats broiled duck or the eggs of wild geese and birds dipped in oil.

Salmon live in the ocean in winter, but they come up the river every summer, to lay their eggs, or spawn. Baby salmon are hatched from the spawn. When they are grown the baby fish go to live in the ocean.

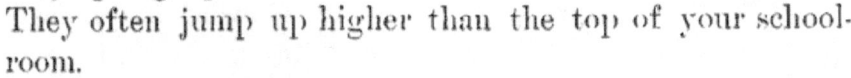

When the salmon come to a waterfall they spring up over it. They often jump up higher than the top of your schoolroom.

The salmon in Alaska die after they have spawned, and the bears feed on them. The Alaskan fishermen try to catch the salmon when they first leave the sea.

They spread great nets near the mouths of the rivers. This net is more than two yards wide and ten rods long. At the top of the net there are blocks of wood that will float. At the bottom are heavy stones tied into wooden hoops to keep the bottom of the net down.

The net is stretched between two canoes. When the nets are full, the canoes are paddled slowly toward the

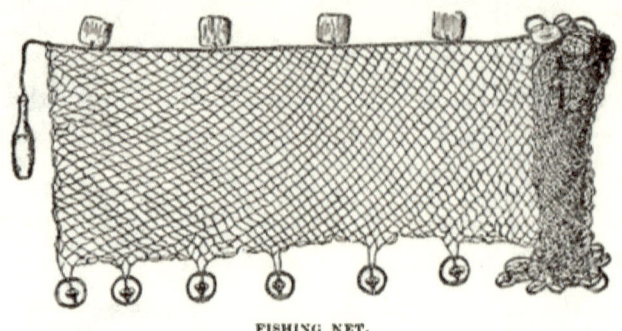

FISHING NET.

shore. Many men help drag the net to the shore.

They do not like to catch salmon with a hook. Sometimes a part of the river is so full of salmon that you can scarcely see the water. What is the largest river in the world, and where is it?

The mouth of the Yukon river is twenty miles wide. The Indians can catch more salmon than white men. They sell their fish at a factory a few miles away. Did you ever eat canned salmon? Chinamen are brought from San Francisco to work in the factories.

In some rivers where a net cannot be used, the Indians spear the fish. They fasten a spearhead to a long stick, and spear the fish very fast.

All spear-heads were once

made of bone. Now the Indians use strong steel fishhooks made in New England.

An Indian always carries a salmon club. Two or three large salmon might tip his light canoe over if they were put into it alive. Before taking a salmon into his canoe the Indian strikes it on the head with a club.

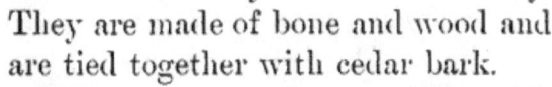

He has a different club for every kind of fish and for every kind of animal that he kills. He thinks it would bring him bad luck to use the wrong club.

Kagoorack is an Eskimo. In the summer the Eskimos go with their families to fish on the islands.

Some of the halibut that they catch weigh a hundred pounds each.

Some of their fishhooks are very odd and clumsy.

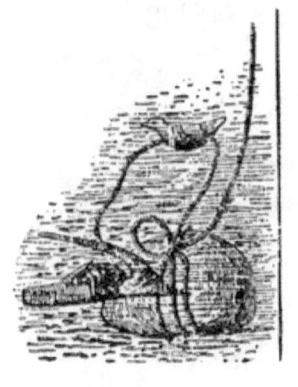

They are made of bone and wood and are tied together with cedar bark.

Indians can catch more fish with these clumsy hooks than our people can with their steel hooks. Kagoorack ties his bait over the point of the hook.

Halibut live near the bottom of the sea. Kagoorack uses a large stone to sink his line. He fastens the line about the stone with a slip loop.

A wooden duck is tied to the line between the stone and the hook. The wood will keep the hook off the bottom.

When Kagoorack has caught a fish he can pull the loop out and draw up his fish without the stone. He will kill the halibut with his halibut club before he takes it into his canoe.

Sometimes Kagoorack fishes for codfish. He uses very queer hooks. They are whittled from knots of hemlock, and bent together after they are steamed. Kagoorack keeps the ends of the hooks tied together.

When he wishes to use one he unties it and puts a little peg between the ends. When a fish nibbles the bait it will knock out the peg, and the hook will spring together and catch it. The peg will come floating to the top of the water to tell Kagoorack that he has caught a fish.

Kagoorack often ties a hundred of these spring hooks to one line. He drops a stone sinker and a wooden bird floats at each end of the line.

When seventy-five or eighty pegs have come to the top of the water he draws up his line. But he does not always draw up as many fish.

If a shark passes by, Kagoorack finds many of his codfish eaten all but the head. Don't you think the shark must like to find a whole line of fish caught where he can eat them so easily?

When Kagoorack catches redfish he uses two hooks.

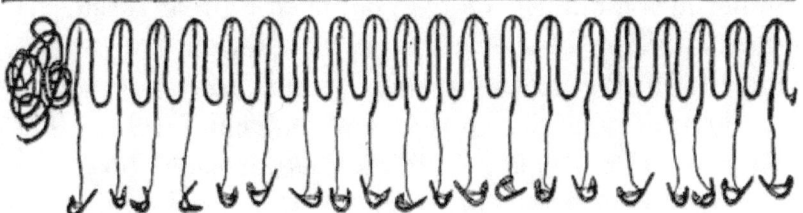

They are fastened at each end of a strong twig. Do you see the twine he uses to tie the bait to the hook? He

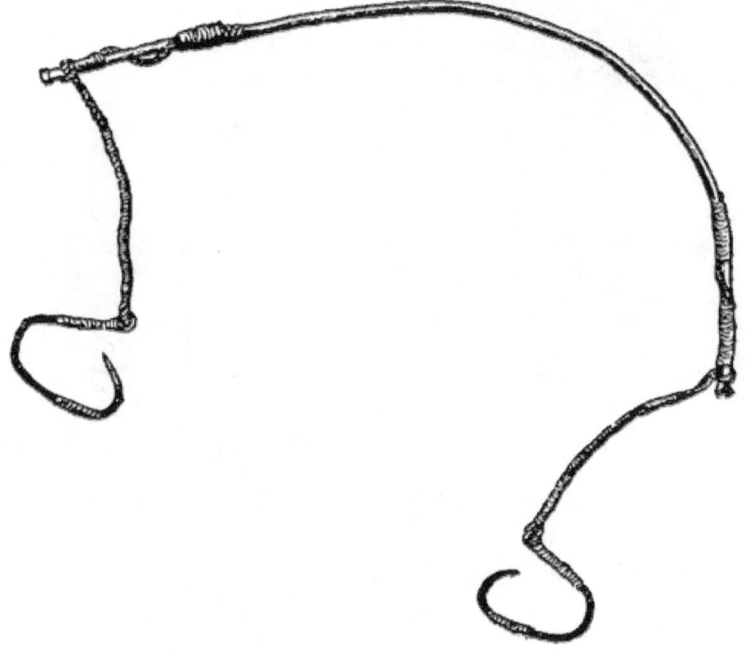

always keeps his bait string wound neatly around each fishhook when it is not in use.

Sometimes a chief calls his people to a great feast. His helper is dressed in a bearskin to look like a real bear.

They will give an entertainment, and the chief and his helper will act out the stories that the chief tells. They will wear different masks and clothes for each story.

The people will sit in front of the stage and listen.

THE CHIEF AND HIS HELPER.

The chief will go behind a small curtain made of blankets to change his costume.

When the people like the story they will grunt, and when they think it is funny they will laugh and shout. Many of the chief's stories will be about bears, and some of them will be told to make fun of white men.

Sometimes the white men have stolen from the Indians,

but other white men are doing many kind things for them. The people like to hear the chief tell about these things.

The people are dressed in their best clothes, for after the chief has told his stories there will be a dance. Many of the people have queer rattles.

One looks like an Indian's head and has real shells for teeth. Another looks like a bird with two heads. Another is a judge with his right hand raised, to make fun of some white man.

Perhaps one will be a whale. The dance is begun slowly, then it grows faster and the dancers shake their rattles.

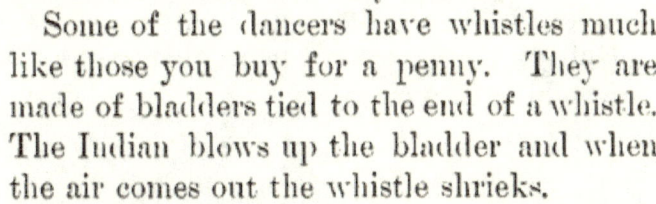

Their bodies sway back and forth and from side to side. They do not move their feet very much.

Some of the dancers have whistles much like those you buy for a penny. They are made of bladders tied to the end of a whistle. The Indian blows up the bladder and when the air comes out the whistle shrieks.

One of the Indians has a great drum made of sheepskin which is stretched over a wooden frame or hoop. The Indian beats it with sticks covered with bird skin.

Some one will have trumpets made of horn. They dance until the chief blows a whistle.

This whistle is called the bad spirit of

the mountains. Whenever it is blown there will be a potlatch. At a potlatch every guest receives a gift.

The potlatch is like your Christmas parties. The gifts are very different from your Christmas gifts.

The wealthy Indians each have three or four blankets given to them. Others receive chests of oil, mirrors, skins, furs, guns, or canoes. The poorer Indians receive a spoon or a spear-head.

Don't you think you would like to go to a potlatch? Every chief must give one once in a while, or people will not think him a great man.

At one of these potlatches the chief's son is made a chief. Then he is a man and not a boy. He must show it by drinking a great spoonful of fish oil without stopping.

The handle of the spoon is carved to look like a fish. The spoon holds a quart of fish oil.

Did you ever see a spoon that would hold a quart? How old will you be before you will be called a man or a woman?

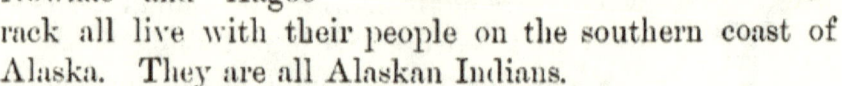

Tipoochac and Nownac and Kagoorack all live with their people on the southern coast of Alaska. They are all Alaskan Indians.

They live in hunting lodges or fishing camps away from the ocean a little while each year. But their real homes are in villages on the coast.

ALASKA. 41

Marchan is a little Eskimo girl with a dark skin and black hair and eyes. She lives in the northern part of Alaska, where it is very cold even in summer. All the Eskimos' names have meanings, and Marchan's name means a sweet root. Where she lives the sun shines all the time in midsummer.

In midwinter there is no sun for a few weeks. Would

A FAMILY OF ALASKAN INDIANS.

you like to live where the sun shines every minute for six or seven weeks? If you had no clock how would you know when to go to bed?

Marchan could tell you. Of what are Marchan's clothes made? What kind of shoes do her people wear?

Long ago the Eskimos always dressed in costly furs. Now they sell the best furs to the white men.

Have you read of Eskimos who build their homes of blocks of ice? They use ice because no trees grow where they like to live. No trees grow in the northern part of Alaska, because it is so cold.

Some houses are covered with sods. Other houses are made of logs and planks; where does the wood come from? The ocean brings plenty of wood to these Eskimos and throws it upon their shores, and they build their houses of the driftwood and cover them with sods. This makes their villages look like a group of many little hills.

But in each hill you will find a door. Climb into the door and you will find yourself in a long entry. There are little cupboards dug into the earth on each side of the entry.

This little girl keeps her playthings in one of these cupboards. She has a bow and an arrow and a small spear, and many queer things that have been washed ashore from wrecked vessels.

Marchan likes to play football, and all the little girls in her village play with her. They use a ball made of snow. One girl will kick it into the air and another girl will kick it up again before it touches the ground. Each girl tries to run where she can kick it as it comes down.

Sometimes they draw a line on the ice and play on sides. If the snowball touches the ground on Marchan's side of the line her party is beaten. When it touches the ground on the other side Marchan will laugh and shout.

Very often the girls keep the ball from touching the

ground for a whole hour by kicking it. Do you think you could do that?

When they are tired of football they play blindman's buff. They draw a circle on the ice, and no one can go outside that circle. They tie a strip of leather over some one's eyes. Then they play blindman's buff just as you do, and when they are tired of that they toss balls in the air. Marchan can keep three balls in the air at once.

MARCHAN'S HOME.

Come into Marchan's home. You will have to climb through a small, high door as if you were climbing into a window.

Marchan takes off nearly all her clothes because she feels very warm in the house. You and I would think it very cold. The Eskimos eat raw fat meat and drink all kinds of oil. That makes them very warm, so that they do not feel the cold.

Two families live in Marchan's home. The bed is a

long bench which slopes down toward the wall. They all sleep on this bed, between deer skin blankets.

Her people have no glass to put into their windows, but they stretch thin skins over a frame. This will let in some light.

In winter, when it is dark, Marchan's mother keeps the lamp burning brightly all day. Her lamp is made of soapstone; do you see it? It is more than half a yard long, and along the front edge she fastens a wick made of moss.

The middle of the soapstone block is hollowed out like a bowl, and it is filled with seal or whale oil. These lamps burn brightly and make very little smoke.

Sometimes Marchan trims the wick with a little stick. Her mother hangs a lump of fat above the flame, and as the fat melts it will drop into the lamp and keep it full.

There is a rack like a small ladder near the lamp, where Marchan's father hangs his mittens or boots to dry. The other family that lives with Marchan's people have a rack and a lamp too.

There is another flat rack near the lamps, on which fresh snow is kept. A wooden tub stands under the rack, and as the snow melts, water drops into the tub, and they drink this water.

Everything is kept very clean in this home. The wooden trays and dishes are rubbed with snow and the horn spoons are kept bright. Even the floors are scrubbed with dry shark skin, and the men must brush their clothes before they come in.

Marchan's mother cooks their food in a small dark room dug in the earth, and this room has a hole in the roof for the smoke.

Back of the house there is a high stage. They put their furs and skins on top of this stage, where the dogs cannot get them. The dogs are always hungry and will eat skins. Marchan goes out and picks up the small pieces of drift-wood for her mother's fire.

Sometimes she finds that the ocean has brought up a large tree that has come from some forest in California or Oregon. Her father will be very glad to get it, and his dogs will help him draw the log home.

Sometimes when Marchan's father is far away from home he builds a snow house to live in for a few weeks; but he builds this house square, and not like the Eskimo huts in Iceland.

In the snow house he makes a square fireplace. It is built of blocks of ice standing on edge, and across the top there is a stick on which he hangs his kettle. He does not build a very hot fire. It is so very cold outside that his ice stove will not melt very much.

In summer Marchan cannot live in the frame house covered with sods, for when

TOTEM POLE.

the snow begins to thaw, the water runs into her house. Then her father will put up a tent near the winter home. Long ago the Alaskans covered their tents with deerskins or bearskins.

Step into my boat and we will go fishing. You may take the spearing fork. We must keep a fire blazing.

When a salmon comes up to the light, spear him quickly. If he tries to get away I will take the net and help you.

MEXICO.

I have three brothers and four sisters. We live with our father and mother in the city of Chihuahua.

The houses are all built close to one another in our city. This makes a wall of houses on each side of the street.

CHIHUAHUA.

Each house is built around a square garden full of beautiful flowers. You can smell the flowers as you come up the street. You can hear the parrots laughing and talking. There are parrots and birds in nearly every garden.

Come, we will go into our house. The door is so large that my father could drive into it. In the large door is a smaller one that we can use.

Come up on the roof and you can see the whole city. Do you see any cottages? The walls are built around the edges of the roof because we often sleep on our roofs when it is very warm.

FAUSTO'S FATHER.

Our bed is made of poles tied together with rope. If we are cold in the night, father spreads his serape over us.

A serape is a woolen scarf which he wears over his shoulders. Sometimes he ties it around his waist.

The girls sleep with mother, and they creep under her reboza. Yes, her reboza is that thin shawl which she wears over her head and shoulders. She is watching for a water-carrier to bring water for our breakfast.

We do not have to dress in the morning, for we do not undress at night. Here comes a water-carrier with water from the best fountain in the city.

Mother has covered her face so that he can see only her eyes. The man fills all her jugs with water, and she pays him for it. He goes along the street calling "Water! water!"

The poor women who have no money are going to the fountain in the street for water. They kneel on the stone curbing and dip their jugs into the fountain. Would

WATER-CARRIERS AT THE FOUNTAIN.

you like to drink water from an open fountain in a city street?

Each woman has a reboza over her head. When she meets a man she draws up one end of it and covers her face so that he can only see her great black eyes.

Mother is making tortillas for us and we will have our breakfast. She grinds the Indian corn between two stones, and mixes it with water and makes it into round cakes.

She cooks them on a flat stone over the fire. Would you like to eat one of them?

You may have honey on it, or I will bring you some

MAKING TORTILLAS.

sugar which grew on my father's farm. We do not have tin dishes. Our dishes are gourds, or jars made of clay and baked in the sun.

Did you ever see gourds growing? They will grow in almost any shape you wish. If you put a gourd that is growing into a bottle it will look like a bottle.

The day before Easter we play a game called hanging Judas. We dress in funny clothes, and then we make a rag doll stuffed with straw. We put firecrackers into the doll's toes and hang him on a line that is stretched across

THE GAME OF HANGING JUDAS.

the street. We light the fuse and push Judas out on the line.

Bang! go the firecrackers, and Judas is all ablaze. We laugh and dance about while he burns.

Three days before Easter we have a carnival. Every boy and girl and man has a bag of flour. We throw the flour at each other and some of us become quite white. The women stay in their houses and lock the doors, and watch us from the roofs.

On the last day we have a battle. The men and boys form two companies and fight each other with the flour.

It flies so thick and fast that you cannot see across the street.

When the boys in our company catch a boy from the other one they take him to the river and duck him. The boy only laughs, and as soon as he can get some dry clothes he joins the game again.

CHRISTMAS BELLS.

Mexican boys do not wear much clothing. In our city they wear shirts and white cotton pants. Where it is warmer people wear only a strip of cloth tied around the waist. Many boys never wear shoes. They wear sandals tied on with strips of leather.

These are the bells which have rung at Christmas for many, many years.

THE PAPER BALL.

I like the game of pinata best, which we play at Christmas time. Early Christmas morning mother makes a great paper ball. She fills it with candies and toys and hangs it from the ceiling. Then we give the baby a stick, and when her eyes are blind-folded she tries to hit the ball.

Enrique is next older and he thinks he can break it. How hard he hits! But he cannot see, so he only hits the air. I am the oldest and must wait till the last. Whack!

goes the stick, and down on our heads tumble all the goodies. I have broken the paper ball, and we scramble for the toys and goodies! We pick up pecans and peanuts and cocoanut snow-balls and toys.

There is peanut candy, and molasses candy, and sugar-

CHRISTMAS MORNING.

cane broken in pieces. I like the great slices of fruit cooked in sugar called dulces. Perhaps you would call it candied fruit.

Here comes a man who lives in a village twenty-five miles away. He has a crate on his back, full of jars and jugs which he has made. There is a large mat rolled up on top of the crate.

That is his bed. He has walked twenty-five miles with this heavy load on his back. When the jars and jugs are sold he will walk back to his home.

Almost every boy in Mexico has a burro, and I can borrow one for you in five minutes. Can you throw a lasso? You would learn to throw a lasso as soon as you learned to walk if you lived in Mexico.

BURROS.

Little Enrique can lasso his dog. He borrows his mother's clothes-line and plays with it until he can throw it over a stick. When he can lasso the stick he tries to catch the dog. The dog runs and Enrique tries to throw the lasso around one of his legs.

When he is a little older he will lasso the chickens and pigs and goats. We play with the lasso until we can catch any animal that runs while we are riding on our ponies.

Some burros can go very fast, but very often they stop and will not go another step. These burros are carrying great loads of wood.

We will stop here, for this is a part of my father's hacienda. A hacienda is a large farm.

You would have to ride twenty miles to drive around it. Would you like to go in and walk through the fields?

A MEXICAN HOME.

We live in this fine house, with bells in the tower to call the people to work. The people who work on the farm live in odd little huts with thatched roofs. Many of our fences are made of cactuses in Mexico. Do you think any one could creep through these fences or climb over them? These cactuses are set near together, and are covered with needles that are long and sharp.

Father will let us each take a pony, and we will go over to a lake that is on his hacienda, and shoot wild ducks.

My little cousin Juan will go with us. He is only eight years old, but he can ride very well, and no horse can throw him off.

When we shoot a duck he will gallop to where it has fallen and reach down from the saddle and pick it up. When a duck falls into the pond, his pony will swim out to it.

My father would like to have us take dinner with him. He says that the coffee and sugar and meat and fruit and vegetables on the table are all raised on his hacienda.

BRANCH OF COFFEE TREE.

We have corn bread and chicken, lamb, rice, bananas, oranges, pineapples, strawberries and melons. Did you ever see coffee or sugar or oranges growing? Can farmers raise them where you live?

Come and see the coffee grove.

Do you see the fragrant white blossoms and the ripe berries on the same tree?

Coffee berries are dark red when they are ripe. The tops of the trees were cut off when they were young, to make the branches spread.

Here is a picture of a branch of my coffee tree. I pick the berries when they are ripe. I picked twenty-three pounds of berries from my tree last year.

Sometimes I find wild orange or lemon or coffee trees growing in the forest, but I never find wild apple trees or wild cherry trees, as you do.

Apples and pears will not grow in Mexico, for it is too warm.

Coffee and oranges cannot grow where there are frosts.

I will tell you how we spread them to dry. There is a high wall

ORANGES.

all around the place. The berries will be turned every day until they are brown. The wall is higher than a man.

We need high walls and good fences, for there are many thieves in Mexico. When the berries are dry we pound them with a mortar and pestle. That will break away the outer husk and leave the seeds. The seeds are the coffee beans.

4

Now we will go through the orange grove. How sweet it smells, and how large the yellow oranges are! You may have as many as you can eat.

I will pick you some orange blossoms, too. You will find these oranges better than those you buy at home. That is because the oranges must be picked when they are green, and left to ripen on their way north. The sunshine makes these oranges sweet.

My father's tobacco field is back of the house. Did the Europeans teach the Mexicans to use tobacco? Which nation used tobacco first?

TOBACCO PLANT.

In the evening my grandfather will tell us stories of the great games the Mexicans played long, long ago. The one I like best was called the flying game. They played it before Columbus discovered America.

The young men cut down a tree and cut away all its branches. They made steps of rope.

A square frame was fastened to the top by ropes. Four other ropes were fastened to the corners of the frame and wound around the pole. When it was all ready, four men dressed to look like hawks or eagles in clothes made of feathers.

They climbed up the rope steps and each one took one of the ropes and swung off.

Another man whirled the square frame around. This unwound the ropes, and made the men fly around and around in larger and larger circles until they reached the ground.

Only men who were strong could play this game. While the flyers were coming down, a man stood on top of the pole and waved a flag and beat a drum. I should have liked to see the men, dressed as birds, play this game, wouldn't you?

MEXICAN IDOL.

These stone images are idols. Do you think a stone god could help you if you were in trouble? The Mexicans were superstitious and worshiped this idol many years ago.

They were afraid of the steam-engine when the railroads were first built. "We do not want that iron horse to come rushing through our country," they said.

But the engine came, with its train of cars. "We will stop it," they said, and they set their stone god between the rails. "Our god will stop the trains," said the Mexicans. "He will kill the iron horse."

On came the train! It struck the stone god and broke it into many pieces and went on.

WAR GOD.

The poor people in Mexico had gods made of wood and clay. The rich people had gods made of silver and gold, for there are gold and silver mines in Mexico. They prayed to one for rain or sunshine, to another for health, and to another for riches.

When they went to war they sang a song to the war god. Do you know any war songs? The Mexicans chanted this song from sunset to sunrise:

Our war god is the greatest god!
No one, no one, is like unto him!
I sing his praises dressed in the dress of our ancestors.
I shine; I glitter.
He is a terror to evil doers; he alone destroyed our enemies and
  conquered them.
When the Dart-hurler shouts aloud he terrifies all the
  people.
Come with me all ye old men and strong men and
  little children, and gather yourselves together
  with me, against your enemies.
Gather yourselves together with me!

Are your war songs like this one? My father's father was a warrior. He carried a copper shield trimmed with feathers, and

SHIELD.

wore a mask over his face when he went into battle.

Do you think an Indian could shoot an arrow through this copper shield? Could a warrior cut through it with this sword? This sword could be used like a hatchet.

The Indians have very strong bows. Sometimes they poisoned the feathers on their arrows, and their arrow-heads were made of stone.

WATER JUG.

SWORD.

Would you have liked to be a Mexican warrior in those old days?

Come into our house, and I will show you a water-jug that is very old. I will put water into it and you may pour the water out of the man's mouth. We must be careful not to break it, for old Mexican jugs and jars break easily. They are made of clay and are baked in the sun. The sun is very hot, but it is not hot enough to make them hard and strong. How are the jugs baked that you have at home? Could you make clay jugs like these? Long ago Mexicans wrote stories in pictures. Here is a vase with a picture story on it. Can you guess what the story is about? I think the man with the cup in his hand is the king.

A PICTURE STORY.

Come and see the picture story on this stone. Can you read it? I cannot, and only a few men can read these picture stories. I study from books very much like yours, but in my school each boy studies his lesson as loud as he can shout. Our teacher has a stick, and if we do not shout loud she strikes the floor.

Could you learn a lesson in a room where all the boys and girls were studying aloud?

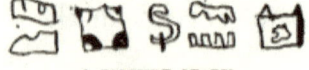

A PICTURE STORY.

Here are more jugs that were made long ago. Mexicans need many jugs and jars because they bring their water a long distance. How far do you have to go for the water that you use at your house? Can you have all the water you need?

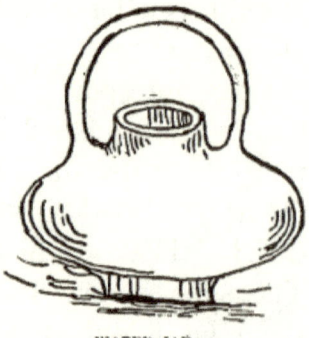

WATER JAR.

Where does the water you use come from?

There are two kinds of farms in Mexico, the fenced farms and those not fenced. My father's farm has a fence around it. Where there are no fences the horses and cattle are

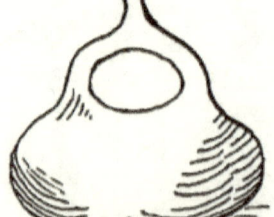

WATER JAR.

branded, and men are hired to ride over the great farms and take care of them.

These men are called cowboys. They always have a lasso on their saddles. When one horse is leading the others away a cowboy rides after them and lassos the leader. A cowboy can ride very fast, and no horse can

COWBOYS.

throw him. The cowboy loves his horse, and his horse learns what his master wishes and obeys him quickly. A cowboy can catch any kind of a horse. He throws the lasso over the horse's head or snaps it around his foot.

When night comes and the cowboy is far from any house he spreads a blanket on the ground and sleeps on it. His horse rests near him and neighs if any wild animal comes near.

In some cities in Mexico water is very cheap, but in many places it costs so much that poor people can buy only a little. We will go to a city where water is scarce.

BEGGAR AND CHILD.

We meet many beggars here, and they are very dirty, for they have no water to wash in. This beggar's little boy is sick. We will give her some money to buy water.

Here comes a rich Mexican, and he will give her some money, too. He is riding on a fine black horse. See the high crown and wide brim of his hat.

A Mexican is always proud of his hat. This man's hat, or sombrero, as he calls it, has a brim eight inches wide, trimmed with silver and gold buttons.

Around the crown of the hat there is a broad silver band which is fastened with gold cords and tassels. This sombrero cost a

SOMBRERO.

hundred dollars. His serape is embroidered with gold and has a silver fringe. His saddle and bridle are trimmed with silver, too.

Fausto told us that he lived in the city. This man lives in the country and is very poor. His boy's name is Ramos.

He says, "Buy a basket, if you please." A Mexican boy is always polite, so Ramos bows low before he shows us his baskets.

He has been trying to sell them all day. He is going

A NATIVE'S HOME.

home now and we will follow him. Five or six miles out from the city, Ramos comes to a village or *pueblo* where the houses are all made of adobe.

Adobe is a kind of mud or clay. He will stop here and beg a drink of water and try to sell his baskets.

Do you see a ladder against each house? If Ramos does not find anyone in the kitchen or stable, he will go up the

MEXICAN PUEBLO.

ladder to the roof. The ground floor is always used for a stable and a kitchen in these houses.

In this part of Mexico the rainy season is six months long. The dry season is between the last of October and the first of May. How long is the dry season?

As Ramos walks on down the rough road he meets

INDIAN CAMP.

men who have been working on farms going home with bundles of oranges or cotton or sugar cane strapped on their backs.

Now Ramos is passing an Indian camp. The tents are made of skins thrown over poles which have been put into the ground.

These camps are called Indian tepees. The Indians of Mexico live in one place a long time.

The Indians love their homes. This mother is feeding her children from the kettle of soup she has made for them.

She has made it thick by putting in pounded beans. Would you like a spoonful of it?

MEXICAN OX CART.

Do you see this Mexican cart? It is drawn by oxen. They wear a great yoke on their necks. Are the wheels of the cart made like wheels you have seen?

This is Ramos's home, and his father and brothers and

sisters are waiting for him. Mexicans love their children and are very kind to them. Ramos has fifteen brothers and sisters, so they all have to work.

When a boy is only seven years old he can walk ten miles to a city to sell the baskets or toys that his mother has made, and then walk home. Mexican boys never

RAMOS'S BROTHERS AND SISTERS.

hurry, but they work very steadily until their work is done.

There is no chimney on Ramos's house. The Mexicans do not need chimneys, for all the cooking is done out of doors. Ramos's father works for a farmer who lives near.

The farmer harnesses his horses and drives to the city.

His wife rides in the carriage with him. She does not wear a reboza. She wears a beautiful lace scarf which she made herself.

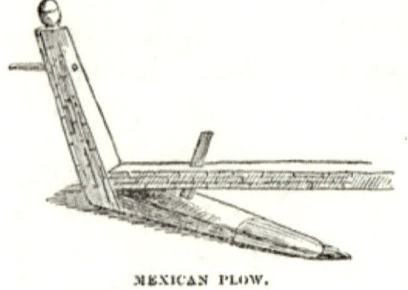

MEXICAN PLOW.

Did you ever see a farmer plowing? This is the plow that Ramos's father uses. It has only one handle, and he holds the plow with one hand and drives the oxen with the other.

A Mexican will not buy a plow with two handles. How do farmers plow where you live?

The city of Mexico is the capital of Mexico. Ramos walks many miles to church. He goes to the largest church in America. It is in the city of Mexico, and

THE CATHEDRAL OF MEXICO.

Ramos is very proud of the beautiful cathedral. He will tell you that it took a hundred years to build it and that it cost five million dollars. He is very poor, but he always brings a little money to the church.

Ramos likes to look at the beautiful carvings on the wall and at the great bronze doors. The altar rail is of silver and copper and gold melted together. The altar is of solid gold trimmed with silver. The priest's robes are made of gold thread woven together and embroidered with jewels. On his way home Ramos kneels and worships again at a wayside shrine.

"Push your boat swiftly along, if you please, Mr. Gardener. We are waiting to buy some of your great strawberries and pine-apples for supper. We know they will be the best in the world, for you are bringing them from the floating gardens."

The floating gardens are islands which are in a pretty lake near the city of Mexico. These market gardeners are coming down the Viga canal, which has been made between the lake and the city.

Their gardens are very fine because there is always plenty of water near, even in the dry season. Come quickly, for we want to buy some of your fruit and flowers!

Oh, what beautiful pansies! They are as large as the top of a cup, and the poppies are as large as dinner plates! The pansies are yellow and violet, and the poppies are bright red and yellow. Do you like such pretty flowers?

This is a strange place, but Ramos likes to come here. It is the Thieves' Market. Every Sunday morning the thieves come here to sell what they have stolen.

They put up crazy looking umbrellas or tents and spread

THIEVES' MARKET.

out their goods. "Come and buy," they say, "for we can sell cheaper than anyone else."

There are more thieves in Mexico than in almost any other country.

What do the police do with thieves where you live?

Do they let them sell the things they have stolen where everyone can see them?

Isn't this a strange farm? It is a few miles from the city of Mexico. "What are you raising on your farm, Mr. Farmer?" These plants look like century plants, which we often see on lawns and in gardens in the United States.

Why do they raise so many century plants? The drink that Mexicans like best comes from century plants. We call it pulque.

CENTURY PLANTS.

When the century plant is ready to blossom a shoot comes up which grows as high as your school-room.

I do not see any tall stocks.

No, the men have cut them down, and have hollowed out the stump that is left. See, here is a hollow as large as a water pail. Is that water in it? No, that is the sap which would have fed the stock, and it fills the hollow every day.

This man has come to take away the sap. He has a long gourd with a hole in each end of it. He dips one end into the sap and sucks at the other end until the gourd is full.

MAN WITH PIG SKIN COLLECTING PULQUE.

He empties the gourd into the pig skin on his back. How is the pig skin fastened to him? How will he get the pig skins to the city when they are full?

Do you see who is waiting to carry them for him? Mexicans like pulque best when it is old and sour. You would not like pulque.

Do you have cocoa for breakfast? Did you ever hear of trees that needed a sunshade?

You see two kinds of trees in a cacao grove. Cacao trees must be shaded from the sun. Banana trees are planted among them. The banana tree will grow tall very fast and will spread its great leaves over the cacao trees like an umbrella.

Men with long forked sticks will knock down the cacao pods and Ramos will catch them or pick them up. The cacao pods are as large as cucumbers and have many seeds.

The men crack open the pods and take the seeds out with a wooden spoon. The seeds look

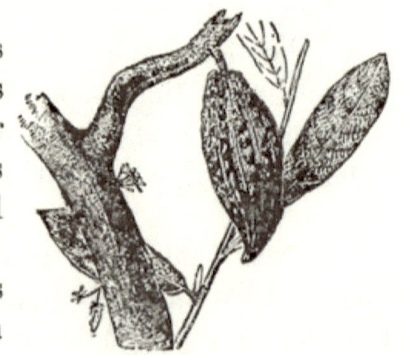

BRANCH OF CACAO TREE.

like almonds. Inside the shell there is a soft pulp that is good to eat.

The cacao seeds are buried in the sand five days, when they are taken out of the sand and roasted.

Ramos's father plants a great field of flax.

When it is grown the blossoms are blue. When the blue petals fall off the seeds will change into a small brown ball. The stalks and stems of the flax are made into linen fibre. The lint is spun into linen thread, and the thread is made into strong cloth.

Ramos's mother spins her own flax. She makes it into very fine linen. Another woman takes the linen and draws out some of the threads and makes beautiful table covers. Did you ever see any Mexican table covers?

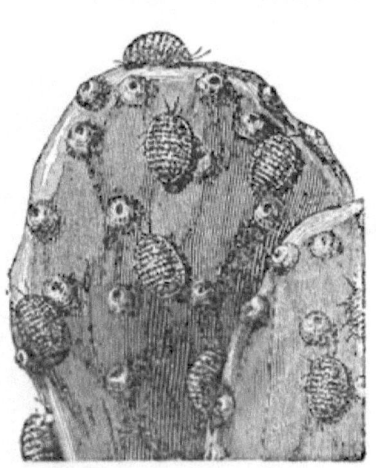

COCHINEAL INSECTS ON CACTUS LEAF.

What color do you like best? The Mexicans like bright red. They dye the linen red with dye that is made from a small insect. The insect is called a cochineal bug. It feeds on the cactus. Ramos brushes the brown cochineal bugs into a dish and takes them home to dry. His mother makes a dye of the bugs.

What a strange hill! It is the shape of a pyramid, but trees are growing upon it. That is because it was made by men.

Long ago some Mexican tribes conquered other tribes and made them their slaves. These slaves were made to pile up bricks, one at a time, until they made a great pyramid.

The pyramid covers forty-four acres of land. It is made of sun-baked bricks and is covered with adobe. After

THE VOLCANO OF POPOCATEPETL.

many years trees and vines and cactuses grew all over it and that is why it looks like a hill now.

Come to the top of the pyramid and you can see the volcano of Popocatepetl. What is a volcano?

From this volcano we can see another great white mountain. The Mexicans think the top of this mountain looks like a woman asleep. Its name means "The White Woman."

CRATER OF THE VOLCANO POPOCATEPETL.

NORWAY AND SWEDEN.

See how the goats and chickens come to meet us! All the animals on a farm are treated very kindly in Norway

A NORWEGIAN FARM.

and Sweden. The cows and the horses will come to you.

The hens and ducks follow us like playmates, for no one has ever hurt them. They think every boy and girl likes them. This farm is a way station. There are not many railroads in this country. How can we travel here?

We can hire a cariole and be driven down the mountain roads in it. As a cariole will hold only two people, you must have one cariole and I must have another.

A girl drives and she will need one seat in the cariole. She will drive us to the next farm station, then another girl will drive us to another station.

At these farmhouses we can find good food and warm beds. They are much like hotels. Do you think there is room for a trunk?

No, you can carry only a light bag. We cannot take many clothes with us when we travel where there are no railroads.

The roads from one farm station to another are very good ones. They never go over the mountains, but always wind around and between them. Our pony trots along very briskly. Don't you think this is a fine way to travel?

The farmer has built a great fire of juniper and fir branches under the oven, and his wife is making rye-bread. She will bake enough at one time to last all through the harvest.

Is she making the bread into loaves? No, she has rolled it into thin, round cakes, and it looks like the top crust of a great pie. She will put it on a long-handled griddle, and then she will bake it hard. This is the bread we like best in Sweden.

A hole is made in the middle of it, and it is strung on a long pole, which is hung from the ceiling.

SKED.

The Swedes do not eat the bread when it is new. They say new bread makes people sick; old bread makes them strong. You must have good teeth if you wish to eat a piece of Josephina's bread.

Soon the grass will be green, and then we shall take our cows up into the mountains. We have many pastures for our cows among the mountains.

We live there all summer. These pastures are fifty miles from our home on the farm, and you will not care to go with us, for the road is steep and rocky.

Father comes to see us only twice each summer, and then he brings us what we need from the farm. We are too busy to be very lonely, for we must watch the cows so that the wolves will not kill them. The cows eat the grass which grows between the rocks. All the grass which grows on the farm must be saved for winter.

We drive the cows to a new pasture once every week. They always know their way back. There are dairy huts near the one that we live in. Do you know what is done in a dairy?

Yes, we make butter and cheese there. When father

NORSE TOOLS.

comes to visit us he will take home all we have made, and he will sell it at the market. We make many, many pounds of butter, and this is the way we earn most of our money.

Do you go away to spend the summer? Do you go to work, or to have a good time? When a cow gets lost we blow our horns, and she comes quickly when she hears them. Our cows are always gentle and they like to follow us, for we pet them every day.

We sleep until we hear them lowing in the morning, and then it is time to get up and milk them.

We set the milk away in the dairy in pans. When the cream has risen we skim it carefully. We make the cream into butter and cheese. Did you ever help to make butter? You may have a great slice of the cheese that we have made if you come to visit us.

It sometimes rains while we are taking the cows to pasture. We hang our wet clothing on poles.

Do you have poles hung from the ceiling of your house? At our house on the farm the poles are carved to look like serpents. We hang the coffee pot and sugar box on these poles.

When washing day comes we take our clothes down to the river and wash them on the stones. How often is your family washing done? We wash twice each year.

LISTENING TO THE STRANGER'S STORIES.

We put on clean clothes every Sunday morning. There will be many, many clothes to wash when washing time comes. It would seem like house-cleaning time to you.

Father has come up from the farm. We are very glad to see him! A stranger has come with him. We will give them the best supper we can cook.

Throw more branches on the fire, and hang the brass kettle on the other crane. After supper we will sit down on the benches and listen to the stranger's stories. Bring out the best bench for the stranger.

Hjlma will work on the mittens she is knitting for next winter. I will sit in the corner and spin.

Long ago there were brave men living in Norway, called Vikings. Hjlma likes to hear about them. Their enemies did not like to see a Viking ship coming.

A Viking wore his ax in his belt, even when he was plowing on his farm. His battle-ax was very large. The Vikings were strong, and cruel to their enemies.

The Vikings would sometimes give the grain they had taken from their enemies to poor people. When an enemy was very brave, a Viking would often give him back half the grain that had been taken.

VIKING PLOWING.

Then the brave enemy would be invited to a feast on the Viking ship. All the brave men would drink from the same drinking horn and after that they were always friends.

The Vikings had strong, beautiful ships. When a Viking chief died they sometimes buried him and his ship together.

DRINKING HORN.

A great cave would be dug, and the ship dragged out of the sea, and put into it. Then every warrior would

VIKING SHIP.

hang his shield on the side of the ship, and a hut was built on the deck.

The chief's body, with his drinking horn, and his sword beside him, was put into the hut. Then all the people of the village put earth upon the ship. When it was covered it made a mound like a small hill.

A few years ago a whole Viking ship was found in one of these mounds.

It was taken to Christiania, and you can see it there to-day. It had sixteen shields, and sixteen places where oars could be used on each side.

The shields are made of pine, and have brass rims. Half of them were painted yellow, and the others were painted black. This is a picture of one of the carved posts.

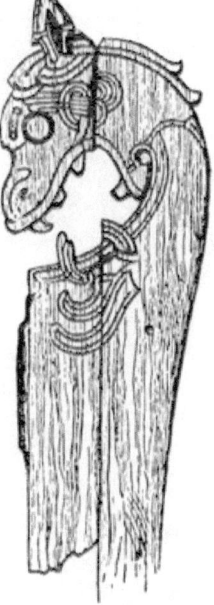

A CARVED POST.

These posts held up the awning which kept off the hot sun and the rain. This Viking ship could carry over seventy men.

There was a great square sail in the middle of the boat. When the wind went down, long oars were used.

The Vikings lived in a cold climate. They were very active, working hard all day. This made them strong and powerful men, so when they used the long oars to row, their ship traveled very fast. Could you row as fast?

THE VIKING'S SHIP, SHOWING THE RUDDER.

This is a picture of their rudder. It was on the starboard side of the ship. Which is the starboard side, and what is the other side of the ship called?

The Vikings were the bravest sailors that ever lived and they sailed around Europe in ships like this one.

One of them sailed over to America many, many years before Columbus discovered it, but he did not know that he had discovered a new country.

Mr. Longfellow has written poems about Vikings. In one of them a Viking tells what he did when he was a boy:

" Far in the northern land,
  By the wild Baltic's strand,
  I, with my childish hand,
    Tamed the gerfalcon.

"And, with my skates fast-bound,
  Skimmed the half-frozen sound,
  That the poor whimpering hound
    Trembled to walk on.

"Oft to his frozen lair
  Tracked I the grisly bear,
  While from my path the hare
    Fled like a shadow."

THE NORTHERN LAND.

A lair is a wild animal's bed. It is usually in some dark cave. What is a gerfalcon? Can you find the Baltic Sea on the map?

CHRISTINA CARRYING MILK.

Christina is selling milk. Don't you think this is a very good way to carry a heavy bucket? Did you ever see boys running with wheels like this? When a holiday comes, Christina wears her hair in two smooth braids down her back.

She wears a bodice made of blue cloth, that she wove herself. It is embroidered across the front with white silk.

Christina works hard all day, but in the evening she loves to dance and sing.

Girls in Sweden and Norway do not wear hats. They pin a handkerchief over their hair in many pretty ways. How do you think Christina knows where a girl lives? She looks to see how she wears the handkerchief on her head.

Did you ever wear a handkerchief on your head in this manner? Try it some time.

Some of the handkerchiefs are very large. Some are small and embroidered with silk.

This is a room in Selma's house.

The bed is put up against the wall. It looks like a great drawer. Selma will stir up the straw that is in it, and will sleep on a blanket spread over the straw.

Her pillow is filled with eider-down. Selma gathered the

CHRISTINA.

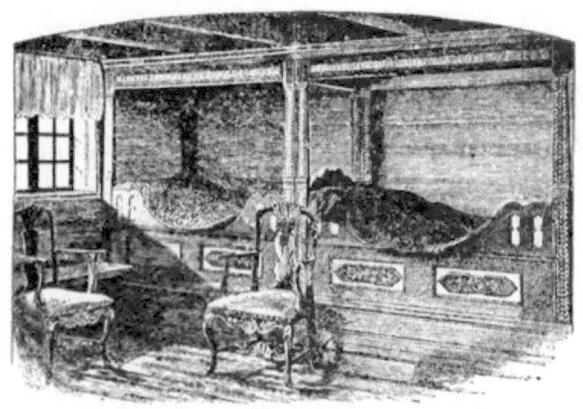

SELMA'S BEDROOM.

eider-down from the eider-duck's nest. There are many, many nests on the rocks near the house. No one ever shoots an eider-duck in Norway, or takes her eggs.

The mother

duck lines the nest with down from her breast. Don't you think her baby-birds have a soft bed?

When Selma takes the down, the mother duck will pick more down from her breast. If Selma takes that, the father drake will line the nest with down from his breast.

When autumn comes, the ducks leave their nests and fly to the warm south. Then Selma will take all the soft white down she can find.

EIDER-DUCK.

When her father goes to the city, he will sell the down at the store and buy Selma some new shoes with the money. Do you sleep on eider-down pillows? Did you ever see a cloak trimmed with eider-down?

Harvest time has come! The grain is ripe and the farmers are gathering it into stooks. Did you ever see a stook of grain?

We are helping in the fields.

When our work is done, the farmer will let us pick up all the scattered straws to carry home. See what large bundles we have gleaned.

Selma carries her bundle on her head. Selma is the

farmer's daughter. The girls who come from the village cannot wear shoes every day.

They go barefoot and save their shoes for Sundays and holidays.

Rich girls and poor girls work together in the field and they are good friends. They sing together as they come down the road.

GRANDMA READING TO SELMA.

If a rainy day comes, Selma will spend it knitting. She is making a pair of stockings for her father. Does some one knit your stockings? Grandma often reads to Selma while she works. Selma listens, and remembers what is read. Does your mamma read stories to you?

Selma learned to knit when she was a very little girl. She can knit very fast without looking at the stitches. When Selma goes to visit some girl who lives four or five miles away, she takes her work, and sings and knits as she rides along the road. These girls keep knitting while they are talking. The balls of yarn and the needles are nearly always in their pockets. They love to knit, and do not think it is work at all.

Rock-a-bye baby. You cannot fall, for the branch will not break. Mother will soon take you home. Your broth-

HARVEST TIME.

ers and sisters will be waiting for you. They have been working in the fields too.

We all work hard at harvest time, for the summer is short in Norway. Now we will have a good supper. We are very hungry after we have been at work in the field, and we go to bed as soon as it is dark.

What do you say when you leave the table? In Norway and Sweden every child goes to the father and mother and says, "Thank you for the food."

Sometimes a stranger is asked to dinner or supper. When he leaves the table he will always go and shake hands with the father and mother and say, "Thank you for the food," too. The people in Norway and Sweden are very kind to travellers. They invite them to come in and rest and give them the best room in the house.

On the cliffs near Selma's home there were once many auks. It was very easy to kill these auks, because their wings were so short they could not fly away easily. Men would drive them together among the rocks and kill them with clubs. Now there are very few auks to be found. Johan wishes that he could see one. He would watch for its eggs and sell them. Do you suppose he will ever find one?

Once there were many birds near our own homes. Now we can find but few nests, and we hear only robins and sparrows and pigeons. What has become of the house wren and the swallows, and where are the bluebirds? Yes, the English sparrows have driven many of them away. What can we do to help to bring back the birds that have left us?

If we put bits of thread and hair and moss where they can find them, do you think they will build their nests near our homes

AUK.

again? We can try to keep their nests safe from bad boys.

Every little egg in a nest is very precious now, for we want to hear the birds singing about us. Each little egg that is broken means that there must be one less bird. Our little bird friends help us, too. They feed on the grubs and worms that would spoil the buds and flowers.

SELMA'S HOME.

Did you ever see a duck egg-dish? You will find one in every home in Norway. We eat a great many eggs and they are always put on the table in a dish that looks like a duck.

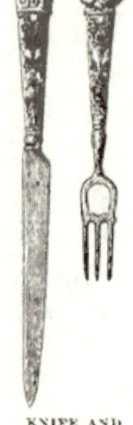

KNIFE AND FORK.

The cover of this dish is made in the shape of a duck. Lift up the cover and help yourself to an egg. You will find that the egg is large. It is not a hen's egg, but the egg of some wild bird.

Johan found these eggs in nests on the rocks. He never takes the eider-duck's eggs, and he will not take all the eggs from any nest. Some day we will go out on the rocks with him. We will take a basket with us and try to bring home enough eggs for dinner. Did you ever hunt for eggs in a farmer's barn? How many did you find?

GETTING A BOAT-LOAD OF HAY.

Come, we will row up the river for a boat-load of hay. We shall need all the hay we can find before winter is over.

Hurry, so that we can load our hay into the boat and pull away before Hans comes! We will laugh at him and make him think he must carry his load home on his head.

Ah, here comes Hans. He does not wish to walk home with his hay. He says that he will jump into the boat from the stepping-stones. Wait, Hans! do not tip our boat over. We will come for you. We were only joking when we rowed out here. Hans will help us row home. We shall need Hans, for he is strong, and we must row against the current.

All summer long we have been gathering hay into our barns. We have brought it home in boats and in wagons. We must save all that we can find before the frost comes. When our cows come home from the mountain pastures where they feed all summer, they will need the hay. Our good cows must never go hungry, for they give us our milk. From the milk mother makes butter and cheese.

Then we must gather a bunch of grain and put it away for Christmas. When Christmas time comes, every family in Norway will tie a bunch of grain to the top of a tall pole and set it out in the deep snow. Soon the birds will come fluttering about to find their Christmas dinner. They will go from one bunch of grain to another and get all the seeds they can eat. After they have had their Christmas dinner, they will come back and sing to us. We love our Christmas birds and are glad to save some grain for them.

GATHERING FLAX.

SELMA'S MOTHER SPINNING FLAX.

We will gather flax to-day. After it is dried we will pound off all the seeds, and spread the stocks on the grass. We will let the dew wet them and the sun shine on them until they are soft. Then we will pound them until we can comb the flax into long fibers. Mother will spin these long fibers into fine threads on her spinning-wheel.

Do you know what we do with the fine linen thread after it is wound on spools? We have a loom in our house, and we shall weave the flax into linen. Our clothes are made of the linen. We pack the linen away in a great chest until we need it. When Selma's wedding day comes, her clothes will be made from the linen that we have put away in the chest.

RAKING UP CLAMS AT LOW TIDE.

SETTING THE SAIL.

The tide is out and we can rake up clams and catch little fish in our nets for bait. When the tide turns we will launch our boat and go fishing.

Do you see our sail? Mother will row while father sets the sail. Mother is very strong. We shall bring home many fish.

We shall have some of the fish we catch for dinner, and we shall sell the others to the men who dry them for the market. Do you ever eat salt fish that has been dried? Perhaps we caught some of the codfish you have eaten.

Our people send great ship-loads of fish to America. Come and see how the fish are dried. Do you see the racks? Can you see the codfish hanging down from the slats that are put across the racks?

DRYING CODFISH.

You would not care to stay near the place where the fish are drying, for you would not like the smell, but we do not notice it. Do you see the schooners waiting to take the fish away? Many men are kept busy packing the codfish in boxes and storing it away on the boats. Other men are out on the ocean catching the fish. Their wives wait at home and watch the weather as they work. They hope there will not be a great storm and a fierce wind. Many strong boats have been dashed to pieces in these storms. We hope that all the boats we see in the harbor will have a safe voyage. Some one will be watching for them when they return. How often does your father come home?

GOING TO CHURCH IN A BOAT.

Do you watch for him? Did you ever watch a fishing-boat come home from sea?

There is no church near our home.

I can see a large boat coming from an island. Every Sunday we row five miles to church in our large boat. Fifty people can ride in many of our church boats.

Do you hear them singing a hymn as they row across the water? Would you like to go to church in a boat? These people enjoy it.

Sit down, Thelma, and I will smooth your hair while you do Selma's. The wind has blown it about our faces as we rowed across the water. We must look very neat before we go into church. We have brought our shoes and our clean linen kerchiefs in boxes. We will put them on and be all ready for church before we go on shore.

Trip, trip, lightly they go, while the music sounds through the room!

In these days the Norwegian boys and girls dance very much as you do. They waltz and polka and dance the square dances. They enjoy it as much as you and I do.

Long ago they danced the spring dance, as this boy and girl in the picture are doing. Gustaf would take Hjlma's hand, and they would trip lightly in their heavy clog shoes. They always kept perfect time to the music. They loved the spring dance and they loved the merry

DANCING IN NORWAY.

music which was always played for it on the violin.

In those days they went barefooted through the week, to save their shoes for the dance. Few people could afford to wear shoes every day. They wore them only to dances and weddings and to church. Would you like to try to dance the old spring dance that Gustaf and Hjlma enjoyed so much? Join hands, spring lightly, and come down each time on the beat of the merry music. Your feet must only just touch the floor. Gustaf and Hjlma often walked many miles to such a dance, and then walked home again.

What strong, brave men! They are carrying King Harold's little son Hakon across the mountains. Hakon's father was afraid his cruel brothers would hurt him.

The brothers wanted to kill him so that he would not have a part of the kingdom when King Harold died. These brave, kind-hearted men went swiftly over the mountains on their snow-shoes.

These men were called birch-legs. Look at them and see if you can guess why. They took Hakon to England in a ship and gave him to the king of England. The king was very kind to the little Norwegian child, and let him grow up with his own sons. Then he sent him back to Norway.

When Hakon became a man he was made king, and he tried to teach his people what he had learned in England. He wanted to tell them about the God whom you worship, but his people would not listen to him.

Many, many years after Hakon died, his grandson made the people listen and they became Christians. This grandson was called Olaf the Glorious. Why was he called that? What did he do?

Sometimes he was called Olaf the Holy. Mr. Longfellow has written some verses about Olaf. King Olaf had a ship built to look like a great sea serpent. When it was done he called it The Long Serpent.

BRAVE NORWEGIANS CARRYING HAKON ACROSS THE MOUNTAINS.

THE BUILDING OF THE LONG SERPENT.

Round him busily hewed and hammered
   Mallet huge and heavy axe.
Workmen laughed and sang and clamored,
Whirling the wheels that into the rigging
   Spun the shining flax.

.   .   .   .

Till at anchor, carved and gilded,
Lay the dragon-ship he builded;
'Twas the grandest ship in Norway,
With its crest and scales of green.

The Long Serpent it was christened,
'Mid the roar of cheer on cheer.

LONGFELLOW.

THE LONG SERPENT.

VALKYRIES' SONG.

The Sea-king looked o'er the brooding wave;
  He turned to the dusky shore,
And there seemed, through the arch of a tide-worn cave
  A gleam, as of snow, to pour;
    And forth, in watery light,
    Moved phantoms, dimly white,
  Which the garb of woman bore.

Slowly they moved to the billow side;
  And the forms, as they grew more clear,
Seemed each on a tall, pale steed to ride,
  And a shadowy crest to rear,
    And to beckon with faint hand,
    From the dark and rocky strand,
  And to point a gleaming spear.

Then a stillness on his spirit fell,
  Before th' unearthly train,
For he knew Valhalla's daughters well,
  The Choosers of the slain!
    And a sudden rising breeze
    Bore, across the moaning seas,
  To his ear their thrilling strain.

"Regner! tell thy fair-haired bride
She must slumber at thy side!
Tell the brother of thy breast,
Even for him thy grave hath rest!
Tell the raven steed which bore thee,
When the wild wolf fled before thee,
He too with his lord must fall,—
There is room in Odin's Hall!"

. . . . .

There was arming heard on land and wave,
When afar the sunlight spread,
And the phantom forms of the tide-worn cave
With the mists of morning fled;
But at eve, the kingly hand
Of the battle-axe and brand,
Lay cold on a pile of dead!

—Hemans.

The Norsemen told their sons that up in the clouds there were noble women mounted on splendid white horses watching them. They said that when a brave man died in battle, these women, who were called Valkyrs, would gallop down to earth and take the brave man, who had been killed, back to heaven on their splendid horses. These noble young women were the handmaidens of Odin, the god of war, who dwelt in Valhalla.

A MODERN NORWEGIAN BOAT.

Some day we will go to Norway and Sweden, and while we may not find any of the old viking's ships, we may find in some of the museums, carved posts, shields, a curious rudder, and other parts which will remind us that these ships once existed and sailed over the north seas.

We shall find many objects of interest there, different from those at home. A boatman will take us in a strong, modern Norwegian boat to the home of the auk, and we will learn the habits of this strange bird. We will hunt for the eggs of the eider-duck, and we will fish for salmon at the mouth of the river.

When the snow comes, perhaps Erik will harness his reindeer to his sleigh and give us a ride over the snow-covered fields. We will visit Selma's home and see all the curious old furniture, and dishes, and plates with odd pictures painted on them. We will buy some of these things for our friends at home.

We will watch Selma's mother spinning the flax into fine linen thread, and perhaps she will make for us some fine linen handkerchiefs with pretty designs woven in.

It is winter and the lake is frozen over. Come and skate with us on the ice and we will take a sail. Put the crossbar on your shoulder and slip your arm under the strap.

Now you need not skate, for the wind will fill your sail and take you two miles down the lake in five minutes. Coming back we shall put the sail on the other shoulder and tack. Do you know what tacking means in sailing?

Do you see how clear the ice is? You can see the bottom of the lake and the fishes darting among the weeds growing there.

Don't you feel as if you were flying? This afternoon I will take you sleighing. Do you have sleighs like ours in your country? How are they made?

IMPLEMENTS OF WAR.

A cruel king once came from Denmark to rule over Norway and Sweden. He invited all the noblemen of the country to a great feast. When they came he ordered his soldiers to kill them.

Then the king thought there would be no one left to

raise an army against him. But one young nobleman named Gustavus Vasa did not go to the feast.

When Gustavus heard how his father and the other nobles had been killed, he wanted to drive the cruel king back to Denmark. He went all over the country asking the farmers and fishermen to help him.

The king heard what Gustavus Vasa was doing and he

COINS.

offered to give a bag of gold to any one who would kill the young nobleman.

The soldiers hunted for him all over the country. They offered to pay any one who would help them. The country people were poor, but they would not take the money.

They helped Gustavus Vasa hide. He wanted to get to Dalarne. Many soldiers lived at Dalarne and he thought they would help him raise an army.

Once the soldiers almost caught him, but he ran into a cottage. A woman named Marget,

COINS.

WARRIOR

who lived in the cottage, opened a door in the floor, and Gustavus went into the cellar.

Then the woman shut down the door, and put her great tub over it, and went on with her work. When the soldiers came they offered her gold if she would help them find Gustavus Vasa. The soldiers did not know there was a cellar under the house, so Gustavus Vasa was saved.

Gustavus once dressed like a servant and worked for a woman in her kitchen. The soldiers looked at him, but did not know him. So Gustavus was saved again.

A NORSEMAN.

Gustavus Vasa went on over the mountains until he came to Dalarne. But when he reached the town, the people said, "We will not fight. We have long been at war. Let us rest." This was very hard for Gustavus to bear when he had come so many miles to find these soldiers. He went sadly away. But after he was gone the men of Dalarne sent men to say, "Come back and we will fight with you!"

So they dressed in their battle cloaks and took their swords and spears and battle-axes, and drove the cruel king back to his own country.

This was long ago, but ever since that time the people have had their own king.

Olaf lives in a hut with his father and mother and brothers, in the northern part of Norway. Do you think it is warm where they live? Why do you think it is cold? Olaf's house is made of poles covered with sods. All around the inside of the hut is a platform made of poles. This platform is the bed. Every one in the family sleeps on this bed.

WARRIOR.

Every one sleeps between reindeer skins. In the morning Olaf's mother cooks some reindeer moss for breakfast. She cooks it in milk and water, and Olaf thinks it very nice.

Olaf's father owns five hundred reindeer, and Olaf helps to milk them. How much milk does a Jersey cow give? Olaf can get only a teacupful of milk from each reindeer, but it is very thick and rich.

REINDEER.

He puts some water with it before he drinks it. He likes it best when it is so sour that it is like jelly. Do you like sour milk?

Olaf helps his mother make cheese from the milk, but reindeer milk does not make good butter. Olaf's people are not Swedes. They are Lapps. Lapps like to live where it is so cold that no trees, flowers, or grass can grow.

WINTER IN NORWAY.

The Lapps own many reindeer. The reindeer like to live in cold countries, and they feed on the moss that grows between the rocks. When the ground is covered with snow the reindeer dig holes and find moss to eat.

Does a reindeer always wear the same horns? How often do the old ones drop off and new ones grow out? Does a cow have new horns every year?

The reindeer can swim across a wide lake. A Lapp thinks he is very poor if he does not own several hundred reindeer. Olaf has reindeer meat for dinner, and drinks

SWEDISH LAPLANDERS.

reindeer milk, and his coat and cap and shoes are made of reindeer skin.

He sleeps on blankets made of reindeer skins. When

OLAF'S SICKLE.

he wishes to go to ride he harnesses a reindeer into a queer little sleigh that looks like a boat. You would fall out of a reindeer sleigh, for it rocks about when it moves.

Reindeer can run very fast. Olaf drives a reindeer with one rein. He throws the rein over one side if he wishes the reindeer to go fast, and over the other side when he wishes him to stop. Olaf goes fishing with his father. His mother will salt and dry the fish they catch.

The fish can then be put away for winter use. Olaf cuts up reindeer moss with this sickle, and then cooks it in milk and water for the little reindeer.

Olaf cannot live very long in one place. When the reindeer have eaten all the moss near his home he must go to another place.

His father finds a good pasture many miles away, and builds another hut.

He ties the tent poles together and a reindeer drags them to the new home.

Why can they not cut new

FISHING IMPLEMENTS.

NORWAY AND SWEDEN.

poles? Olaf helps to drive the reindeer. When they have eaten all the moss within a day's journey of this home Olaf must move again.

Sometimes Olaf crosses a glacier on the way.

What is a glacier? Does it move as fast as a river of water?

Olaf often sees great icebergs in the ocean.

What is an iceberg?

When Olaf comes to open water he often catches fish with spears or nets.

Olaf often sees polar bears running across the ice.

His father shoots the bears and they have bear meat to eat.

They are glad to see the bears, for they are very fond of bear meat. Where does your father get the meat that you eat?

His mother makes long boots that look like stockings out of the white bear skin, and she makes short boots and slippers too.

She turns the fur inside and the boots are very warm.

Would you like a pair of bear-skin boots for next winter?

BOOTS.

ERIK'S HOME.

Erik is a Lapp boy too, but he lives in the mountains. His father's home must be moved very often.

He makes it of poles and covers it with reindeer skins. Olaf always lives near the ocean. The coast Lapps build huts of sods and live on sea-fish and bear and reindeer meat.

The mountain Lapps have tents, and eat salmon and other fish caught from the mountain brooks. Do you ever eat smoked salmon?

There is a big kettle hanging over a camp fire near Erik's home. His mother has made some soup from fish. Erik will eat it with a horn spoon which his father made from a reindeer's horn. In the small kettle you will find some hot coffee. Can you tell where coffee grows?

THE BIG KETTLE.

When the reindeer have eaten all the moss they can find near this place, Erik's people will move. His father will roll up the tent poles in reindeer skins and tie them on a reindeer's back.

He will harness another reindeer to a sleigh for himself and one for each of the children. They will drive to their

A REINDEER SLEIGH-RIDE.

new home, and the hired men will bring the herd of reindeer.

Sometimes the mountain Lapps are driven away from the mountains to the coast in summer. Can you guess what drives them? Do you think it is wolves or bears? No, it is the mosquitoes. The mosquitoes are very large, and come in such clouds that you can hardly see beyond them. They sting the reindeer so that he wants to plunge into the water and get rid of them.

Erik's mother always goes to church when they are near one, and she takes her baby with her. Can you see the baby? Do you know where he is?

Yes, the baby is in that queer bundle in her arms. Just outside the church baby's mother will bury him in the snow all but his head.

The reindeer skins keep him warm. She leaves him there beside the babies that other mothers have brought. The babies will be warm and happy in their snowy beds.

LAPP'S CRADLE.

When church is over Erik's mother takes her baby back to the tent. She gives him his dinner, and then she rocks him to sleep in his pretty cradle.

A Lapp mother always has a pretty cradle for her baby. This one is made of white birch bark, and the bark is covered with pretty figures.

Erik's father made these figures on the cradle with a red-hot iron. The cradle is lined with green cloth, and the green cloth is embroidered with red silk.

When baby is in the cradle his mother covers him with soft little blankets that are made of the skins of hares sewed together.

Erik caught the hares in a trap. "Master Hare, you can run very fast. Your coat is white in winter so that the hunters cannot see you run on the snow. Your skin is brown in summer so that no one can see you run over the rocks. But you must keep away from Erik's traps or you will be caught, Master Hare."

Sometimes at night Erik goes out on the bay with his brothers and sisters in a boat to spear fish. They have a large torch in the bow of the boat.

Mr. Longfellow has given us a few words of a Lapland song. It will remind you of the sound of the wind as it whistles through the pines.

SALMON SPEARING AT NIGHT.

> "And a verse of a Lapland song
> Is haunting my memory still:
> 'A boy's will is the wind's will,
> And the thoughts of youth are long, long thoughts!'"

Don't you think Erik would like to sing this song as he slides down the hills on his snow-shoes? How is he steering himself?

Erik will not wait until it is dark before he goes to bed. Do you know why? Where he lives there are eight weeks each summer when it is light all day and all night.

This part of Norway and Sweden is called the Land of

the Midnight Sun. But in winter there are just as many weeks when the sun does not shine at all. It will be almost dark at noon for a few days in midwinter.

How will Erik and his father see to find their reindeer? That is the time Olaf loves best. When the sun does not come up in the morning it is not dark.

The moon and the stars shine very brightly. The wonderful northern lights then blaze up in the north. The aurora borealis will not be as warm as the sun, but it will give plenty of light. It will be more beautiful than any sunset. Are there any other countries where it is as cold as it is in Lapland? Are there

ERIK.

HAMMERFEST.

any other countries where the sun does not shine for many months?

Hammerfest, the northernmost town in the world, is in Norway. Do you see how the houses are built on the coast? Great rocky mountains are back of the town. Nearly all the people who live in Hammerfest are fishermen.

Beyond Hammerfest is the lonely North Cape. It is the northernmost point of land in Europe. Many travelers climb to the top of the North Cape, but no one lives near there. No trees or shrubs or flowers grow near it. Why do travelers go there?

NORTH CAPE.

(THE DISCOVERER OF THE) NORTH CAPE.

"So far I live to the northward,
No man lives north of me;
To the east are wild mountain chains,
And beyond them meres and plains;
To the westward all is sea.

"The sea was rough and stormy;
The tempest howled and wailed,
And the sea-fog, like a ghost,
Haunted that dreary coast,
But onward still I sailed.

"And then uprose before me,
Upon the water's edge,
The huge and haggard shape
Of that unknown North Cape,
Whose form is like a wedge."

—LONGFELLOW.

Do you like stories and myths about giants and brownies and the golden city of the gods? These are the old Norse legends that children of Norway and Sweden love to hear.

Long, long ago there were no people on this beautiful earth, and Odin, the father god, lived in the golden city called Asgard up among the clouds. His wife Frigg, and their many brave sons and lovely handmaidens, lived with Odin.

One day the father god came down the rainbow and walked about on the earth. "This is a bright, sunny place," he said. "I wish there were people here."

He looked about, and saw a straight strong Ash tree and a graceful young Elm standing near together. He touched the Ash, and made it into a man whom he called Askar.

The Elm he made into a gentle, graceful woman, and called her Embla. Askar and Embla were very happy together on the earth and had many children.

Odin came down the rainbow arch and visited them. Then he began to wish he was very wise, so that he might know how to help the earth children to be happy.

Down deep in the earth there was a well of wisdom. If anyone could drink of its waters he would become very wise. But a fierce giant guarded the well. Odin fought with him three days and three nights. At last Odin conquered, and drank the waters of wisdom.

Then he went back up the rainbow to his home very happy. After that Odin was very wise. He could often conquer the cruel Frost Giants who lived near the city of Asgard.

These great cruel giants troubled the earth children and even stole from the gods. One of them had stolen a cask of grape juice.

Odin made them think he was a poor farmer's boy. He offered to work for one of the giants. Soon Odin found the grape juice and took it back home.

Thor was Odin's brave young son, and Sif was Thor's

beautiful wife. Thor and Sif lived with Odin in the golden hall of the gods, in the golden city of Asgard.

Sif's eyes were blue like the summer sky and they shone like the stars. Her hair was golden and very fine, and when she braided it above her snow-white brow it looked like a sheaf of harvest grain.

One day Thor's wicked brother Loke found beautiful Sif sleeping among the ferns and mosses with her golden hair falling loosely about her shoulders.

"Thor is too proud of Sif and her hair," growled Loke. He stole softly up behind her, and with one sweep of his knife he cut off all the beautiful golden crown of hair.

When Thor came home he found Sif weeping. When he heard what Loke had done, Thor was so angry that every time he spoke, it thundered on the earth.

His eyes flashed so very angrily that it made lightning in the skies. Loke was very much frightened, for he was a coward.

Loke begged Thor not to hurt him, but to forgive him. "Not until you bring Sif a crown as beautiful as the one you stole!" shouted Thor. His voice made the very mountains seem to shake with thunder.

Even the Frost Giants were frightened. Loke ran down the rainbow arch to the brownies, who lived down deep in the earth, and commanded them to make a crown for Sif. He said it must be made of the finest gold and be more beautiful than her own had been.

The crooked little brownies hated Loke, but they had to

obey him. They loved Sif, so they made her a crown of gold as fine as silk.

They filled the crown with magic, so that it would grow to her head and be like her own hair. Loke ordered them to make other gifts for Odin and Thor, so that they would forgive him. Loke boasted that the gods would be more pleased with his gifts than with any gift that could be given them.

But one of the brownies thought he could make a gift which would please Thor more. So he made a magic hammer, and he stole up the rainbow behind Loke and gave it to Thor. Loke laughed at the hammer because it had a short, clumsy handle; but the brownies had put magic into it.

Whenever Thor threw it at an enemy or against the clouds it would return to his hand. Thor liked his hammer better than any gift he ever had. He often drove his milk-white goats over the clouds to throw his hammer at the Frost Giants.

When it lightened the earth, people would say, "Thor is angry; see, his eyes flash fire." And when it thundered, they would say, "Thor is throwing his hammer; hear it strike against the clouds."

SWITZERLAND.

Up among the Alps lives Jeanne. Her house—or chalet, as she calls it—is built of logs and rough boards. How low and broad it is! It is only one story high. See the great rocks on the roof. The rocks will keep the house from being blown away by winter winds.

HOME IN THE ALPS.

There are only a few square windows in the chalet. Inside the house is only one large room. Here Jeanne helps her mother make butter and cheese. In the winter evenings she sits beside the fire and knits stockings.

SPRING! SPRING! HO FOR THE MOUNTAIN SLOPE!

As spring comes on and the warmth of the sun is felt, the snow quickly melts from the mountain slopes and invites the herdsmen from the valley below.

A procession is then formed, consisting of the inhabitants of the village, dressed in holiday clothes and gay with ribbons, with which the animals are also decked. A band of music pours forth its lively strains, and the village pastor pronounces his benediction on the interesting doings of the day.

The cattle, who seem to understand perfectly what is going forward, appear almost frantic with joy at being released from their long imprisonment, and the procession moves upward to the high pasture ground on the mountain side, often at a distance of several miles from the village. The path thither winds through black and solemn pine forests, over roaring torrents, and not unfrequently across glaciers and snow fields.

On reaching the pasture ground, the cattle, each one bearing a bell, range at will over the flowery and fragrant turf.

The herdsmen take up their abode for the summer in the mountain chalets, while their wives and families generally remain below. The cattle are driven in twice or three times a day to be milked, and the process of milking and cheese-making continues almost without interruption all the summer.

CATTLE.

They stay there all summer, Pierre and Jeanne coming home often to bring the large pails of fresh milk. At last the days grow colder and the leaves fall. Then they bring their flocks home.

This is the song they sing as they come down the mountains:

> "Farewell to the pastures
> So sunny and bright,
> The herdsman must leave you
> When summer takes flight.
>
> "To pastures and meadows,
> Farewell, then, once more!
> The herdsman must go,
> For the summer is o'er."

In the summer time this little Swiss girl lives most of the time out of doors. She picks sweet strawberries for supper. She will have yellow cream on her berries, but no sugar.

SWISS GIRL.

She helps take care of the cows and goats on the mountain slopes. Sometimes she wanders far away from the mountain chalet.

When Jeanne's papa or brother Pierre go out to look for her and find her nowhere in sight, they shout loudly, and then listen, and soon they hear the sound of Jeanne's trumpet away up the mountain side, and they know she is safe.

Sometimes the cows stray far away from Jeanne. Then she sounds her trumpet with a peculiar call, sits down, and waits patiently, and after a while the cows, who all know her, will come back to her.

She often goes down to her home in the valley to carry berries, fresh milk, and some nice cakes of cheese to her mother and sisters.

She does not mind the rough walk up and down the mountain, as she always wears strong wooden shoes.

Sometimes in the fall, after the cheese-making is finished, Jeanne straps on her back an odd-looking basket filled with cakes of Swiss cheese, and taking another basket-load in her hand, she trudges off to the nearest market place. She has a table there, and on it she spreads a white cloth and lays out the cakes of cheese in all sorts of attractive forms. She spends the day there, or such part of it as is necessary for the sale of her stock, and then, before darkness comes on, she hastens home again, with empty baskets but full purse. Did you ever eat Swiss cheese? Jeanne and Pierre are very fond of sandwiches made with a slice of cheese and coarse rye bread.

JEANNE GOING TO MARKET.

Although Jeanne lives in the country, away from any town, and spends much time roving through the fields, she is very fond of pretty clothes of bright colors made especially for her Sunday toilet.

How would you like a dress like Jeanne's?

One beautiful summer day some strange men came to Jeanne's cottage door. They were travelers from far over the ocean. One of these men told Jeanne that he had a little daughter at home just her age.

These travelers wanted some one to guide them over the mountains. So Jeanne's brother Pierre said he would go with them to show them the way. Merrily they left the little cottage.

The next day they came back again, bringing Pierre with them. He had fallen and hurt his foot. He had to sit still on the porch for a long time. And what did he do all this time? With a sharp knife and some wood he carved many beautiful things. For many days he worked on the case of a Swiss clock with fine net-work and a beautiful little chalet perched on top. When it was finished he took it to a clockmaker in the city and sold it for a good price, and with the money he bought some pretty Christmas presents for Jeanne. Have you ever seen a Swiss clock like that?

He carved a beautiful chamois one day.

Pierre had seen many chamois on the mountains and had hunted them. Many times he had seen them jump from rock to rock. They can run where you would be afraid to walk. Chamois are afraid of hunters and run swiftly away on their approach, so it is very difficult to capture them.

Have you ever seen a chamois skin? For what is it used, and where does it come from? Why are they so expensive?

HAUNTS OF THE CHAMOIS.

This is not a picture of "little boy blue," but of a Swiss boy. Yes, he is blowing his horn, and can you tell why?

His father is far up on the hillside, but he hears the horn. This is the way he tells his father that supper is ready and waiting.

And where has his father been all day, and what has he been doing?

He has been caring for the goats and sheep.

He brings home large pails of goats' milk, and his family will have warm milk for supper.

SWISS BOY.

SWITZERLAND.

INSIDE A CHALET.

Look at the interior of the home of Pierre and Jeanne. While it is not as fine as your home, they think it is very comfortable, especially when the winter storms begin and the snow is piled deep all through the valley. Pierre's pet cow and Jeanne's pet lamb are quite at home in the chalet.

See the alpenstock which Jeanne's father holds under his arm. He has needed it very much to-day, as he has just come from the slippery paths on the mountain.

In the winter, when everything is buried in snow, it is very convenient to have a large supply of good dry wood. How would you like to live in a Swiss chalet like this?

Come with me and I will show you one of the grandest mountains in the world. This is a picture of Mont Blanc, the highest peak in the Alps. "Blanc" means white, so

CHAMOUNIX AND MONT BLANC, FRENCH ALPS.

this is the white mountain. As we look at this mountain our eyes are almost dazzled with its brightness.

>"Mont Blanc is the monarch of mountains;
> They crowned him long ago,
> On a throne of rocks, in a robe of clouds,
> With a diadem of snow."

As this mountain always wears its cap of white **snow**, has it not been well named? The ice and snow on Mont

Blanc look very near to us. And yet, on mule-back we could not reach it in less than two hours.

HOSPICE ST. BERNARD.

It would take us three whole days to climb Mont Blanc. Here lies the village of Chamounix at the foot of the mountain. Can you see some of the large hotels for travelers?

Welcome to St. Bernard! Here you would be cared for by the kind monks who keep this hospice.

If you are cold you will find warmth inside the great building; if you are hungry you will be fed; and if you are

SWISS BOYS.

sick you will be nursed. Is not St. Bernard a welcome sight after your long climb in the snow?

But how can they have great fires in the hospice, for I see no woods or trees. The monks must send twelve miles, to some of the valleys far below them, to get their fire-wood, and sometimes boys bring it up to them.

Is it always winter here? Yes and no. Snow falls nearly every day in the year. Perhaps the monks would tell you that they have summer during July, August, and September, for then the lake in front of the hospice is not frozen.

This house is much like a great hotel. It is so large that

THE RESCUE.

it will hold three hundred people at one time. Do you see a small building near the large one? If the hospice should burn, this smaller house could be used as a place of refuge by the monks and travelers.

THE STORY OF HECTOR, THE ST. BERNARD DOG.

The little inn had but few guests on Christmas Eve. But near the door a traveler stood, who, with knapsack girt and staff in hand, was all ready for a mountain walk.

The keeper of the inn said to the traveler:

> " Nay, stay to-night, the way is long ;
> Dark clouds are flitting o'er the sky ;
> A storm is brewing, trust my word,
> I hear the raven's warning cry."

WELCOME TO TRAVELERS.

"Nay, press me not," the man said, "for I must get home by Christmas Day."

So he left the inn and started on his way. The wind blew colder and colder, and the snow began to fall.

Night fell, and the traveler had lost his way. He sank helpless to the ground. To stay there was certain death.

In the valley below him is the Hospice of St. Bernard.

"It is a wild night," the monks say. "Let us go with the dogs and save some perishing life."

So, taking torches and ropes, the monks and dogs start out. Soon the dogs are on a scent; the monks follow.

The dogs come to a dangerous pass on the mountain

SIMPLON PASS, SWITZERLAND.

side and wait for their masters. Then, at the command, they creep down the pass, and now they come upon the almost frozen traveler. With the kind care of the monks the traveler will be saved.

But where is Hector, one of the brave dogs? His companions seek him in vain.

They will never find him, for a great mass of snow sliding down the mountain side has buried him. The noble dog Hector has lost his life for another, and has met a hero's death.

How can you cross the Alps? You can go on the railroad train if you wish, but I shall take a carriage trip

LAKE LUCERNE.

across the mountains. Then I can see the snow-covered peaks, the valleys and beautiful lakes.

These roads in the Alps must often be repaired. Great masses of snow and rocks sometimes sweep down and destroy parts of the roads.

I would like to take the route over the Simplon Pass. Then I could see the great roads built by Napoleon.

The soldiers built six hundred bridges. In some places they had to cut away great masses of rock. Can you guess how long it took Napoleon to finish these roads and bridges?

Napoleon's first question to those who were doing this work was, "When can the cannon be sent across the Sim-

MOUNT RIGI.

plon?" There is one large hospice in this Pass. It is much like the Hospice of St. Bernard.

For a few cents we can have a ride in a Swiss boat. These little boats can be found in many places on the shores of Lake Lucerne. Of course we must take a boat ride on this lake, for the view from here is grand.

The steep sides of the mountains rise from the side of the lake. In the distance we can see Mt. Pilate. The Swiss people who live near this mountain would tell you that

10

"Old Pilate" is the clerk of the weather. What does that mean?

> "If Pilatus wears his hood,
> Then the weather is always good;
> If he draws his dirk again,
> We shall surely have rain."

ST. GOTTHARD RAILWAY, SWITZERLAND.

The "hood" is a rain cloud that sometimes hides the top of the mountain. The "dirk" is a thin cloud that cuts the "hood."

As at Mount Rigi, there is a railroad up Old Pilatus. If you look sharply at the picture, you can see the railroad. When you visit Mount Rigi you can leave your alpenstock at home. You can take a seat in a car and ride up the mountain.

This is not one of the highest mountains in the Alps,

MATTERHORN.

but the view from the top is beautiful. It seems strange to take a seat in a car in front of the engine. The engine always pushes the car in front of it when climbing a mountain.

Did you ever ride in an open car before? In this car

you are able to look about you on all sides. The train moves no faster than you can walk, so you have a good chance to see the mountain.

After an hour's ride you reach the top. Now far below you, you can see the rivers that look like ribbons. There

INTERLAKEN AND THE JUNGFRAU, SWITZERLAND.

is Lake Lucerne, that looks to you no larger than a little piece of looking-glass. All around you can see the snow-capped peaks.

Would you like to climb the Matterhorn? Do you know what dangers are ahead of you, and do you know how few have ever climbed that great snow-covered mountain? I can tell you of many travelers who have lost their lives on the Matterhorn.

Climb if you will, but remember that courage and strength are nothing without care. Do nothing in haste, look well to each step, and from the beginning think what may be the end if you make a mistake.

You must have a long and stout rope, a bag of food that will last several days, and an ice pick. You will need something to keep you from falling on the ice and snow. You must wear a pair of heavy shoes with nails on the soles, or a pair of crampons. These crampons can be fastened to your shoes, and the spikes will keep you from falling. Do not forget your alpenstock, for you will need that most of all.

When you and your friends have hired guides you start on your journey. You climb all day up the pleasant green slopes of the mountain. At night you rest at one of the little Swiss chalets.

In the morning, long before the sun comes up, you are on your way again. Soon you come to snow and ice. Now you must walk in single file and be tied up with a rope which will hold you all from falling. Only one man can move at a time. If he should slip he could not slide more than a foot without being stopped by the others.

ALPEN-
STOCK.

You will probably spend the second night in a tent which one of the guides will put up. You will be very lucky if you have no thunder storms, snow storms, or wind storms, or falling stones and ice, to hinder you. It is cold, very

EDELWEISS.

cold! On the third morning you reach the summit of the Matterhorn. Does it seem possible that any one of us could climb it?

From the top you can see mountains, mountains, far and near. You can see all of the highest peaks of the Alps; also the green valleys and many of the pretty lakes and streams far below you.

Do you wonder that these beautiful flowers are Jeanne's favorites? The name of the flower is "edelweiss." Shall I tell you the meaning of the name? "Edel" tells us that the plant is noble. "Weiss" means white, so this is a picture of the noble white flower of Switzerland.

The edelweiss grows high up on the mountains. Jeanne often finds it growing only a few inches from a bank of snow.

CLIMBING TO REACH EDELWEISS.

I have known travelers to risk their lives in order to pick these flowers. Here is a picture of a boy climbing to reach the edelweiss which grows just above him. Why must he have heavy nails on the bottom of his shoes?

What are your favorite flowers? Little Jeanne is very fond of roses. The only roses she ever sees are those that grow wild on the hillsides. Can you tell why they are called alpine roses?

They are reddish and purple in color. They are very pretty with their dark green leaves. Here on the mountain sides Jeanne finds violets and dandelions too. But best of all, she sometimes finds the lovely pink forget-me-nots.

CHAMOIS.

I am the chamois. My home is way, way up on the sides of the Alps. In summer I live very near the snow on the mountains. In winter I come down a little way and live in the woods. I do not enjoy living in the woods, for I cannot then run and leap from rock to rock. I can leap thirty feet; could you do that?

My coat now is of a dark brown color, for it is summer. In the winter I shall wear a pretty gray suit. What do I eat? When I can get them I eat plants and flowers; but in the winter I live on young shoots and the buds of the fir and pine trees.

I belong to a large family. Twenty of us live together, and when we are feeding we have sentinels posted. Do you know what sentinels are?

If our sentinel should hear or see anyone coming to harm us, he would stamp on the ground with his fore feet and give a shrill whistle. Then we should all hurry away to some safer spot.

What is the time? I will tell you, for I have my watch here. Perhaps you would like to look at it, for I do not think you have ever seen one just like it.

Is it not pretty? My aunt brought it to me from Switzerland last summer. It is called a Geneva watch, as it was made in the city of Geneva, Switzerland.

I have seen pretty red, blue, and other colored Swiss watches. Have you ever seen one set with precious stones?

A SWISS WATCH.

I cannot tell you how many, many people in Geneva make watches. All the parts of these watches are made by hand. This takes much more work and time than to make the parts by machinery, as we do in our own country. The Swiss people make beautiful clocks, too.

Here is the city of Geneva where so many watches are made. This beautiful city is on the shore of Lake Geneva.

Look at the Swiss boats. I wish you could see this sheet of very clear water. Visitors come from all parts of the world to visit this city and lake. See the mountains all around the lake.

How glad I am that the day is clear. Now we can see Mont Blanc, always wearing its white cap. I have had friends stay in Geneva some time and not see Mont Blanc at all. From this lake, high up in the mountain, flows the River Rhone.

Perhaps you would

A SWISS GIRL.

like to hear about one of my Christmas presents. I think a great deal of it, for it was brought a long way to me.

Last year one of my friends crossed the ocean and spent many weeks traveling in different countries. She went to see the beautiful Alps in Switzerland. Here she bought

GENEVA.

me a paper-cutter. It is black walnut, and beautifully carved.

A great many people in Switzerland earn their living by carving beautiful things out of wood. On the blade of the paper-knife is the name "Luzern." That is the name of the city in Switzerland where this paper-cutter was bought.

Many other beautiful carved articles are found in all parts of Switzerland.

LAKE GENEVA AND CASTLE OF CHILLON.

THE PRISONER OF CHILLON.

My hair is gray, but not with years,
   Nor grew it white
   In a single night
As men's have grown from sudden fears;
My limbs are bowed, though not with toil,
   But rusted with a vile repose,
For they have been a dungeon's spoil,
   And mine has been the fate of those
To whom the goodly earth and air
Are banned and barred—forbidden fare:
But this was for my father's faith
I suffered chains and courted death;
That father perished at the stake
For tenets he would not forsake;
And for the same his lineal race
In darkness found a dwelling place;
We were seven who now are one,
   Six in youth and one in age,
Finished as they had begun,
   Proud of persecution's rage;
One in fire and two in field,
Their belief with blood have sealed;
Dying as their father died,
For the God their foes denied:
Three were in a dungeon cast,
Of whom this wreck is left the last.

There are seven pillars of Gothic mold
In Chillon's dungeons deep and old;
There are seven columns, massy and gray,
Dim with a dull imprisoned ray,
A sunbeam which hath lost its way,
And through the crevice and the cleft
Of the thick wall is fallen and left;
Creeping o'er the floor so damp,
Like a marsh's meteor lamp:
And in each pillar there is a ring,
 And in each ring there is a chain.
That iron is a cankering thing,
 For in these limbs its teeth remain,
With marks that will not wear away
Till I have done with this new day,
Which now is painful to these eyes,
Which have not seen the sun so rise
For years—I cannot count them o'er;
I lost their long and heavy score
When my last brother drooped and died,
And I lay living by his side. . . .

Lake Leman lies by Chillon's walls:
A thousand feet in depth below,
Its massy waters meet and flow;
Thus much the fathom-line was sent
From Chillon's snow-white battlement,
 Which round about the wave enthralls:

A double dungeon wall and wave
Have made—and like a living grave
Below the surface of the lake
The dark vault lies wherein we lay;
We heard it ripple night and day;
   Sounding o'er our heads it knocked;
And I have felt the winter's spray
Wash through the bars when winds were high
And wanton in the happy sky;
   And then the very rock hath rocked,
   And I have felt it shake unshocked,
Because I could have smiled to see
The death that would have set me free.

NAPOLEON.

Shall we not watch this great snow fight? See the snow fort, how well it is made! And here are a hundred boys fighting. Half of the boys are inside of the fort. The rest of the boys are outside the fort attacking it.

Who is the boy commanding the attack? He is the boy who made the plans for the fort. All the boys do just as their commander tells them. Shall I tell you his name? It is Napoleon Bonaparte, and you shall hear of him again.

Here is a great army about to cross the Alps. The commander looks at the shoes of the horses. They must be put on to stay for some time. Each soldier has food for several days. Who is the commander of this great army?

The commander of the snow fort is now a man and the commander of this army.

"Is it possible," asks Napoleon, "to cross this pass of St. Bernard?"

"Perhaps," the guide replies.

"Forward, then."

All these soldiers must march in the narrow path up the mountains. The line of soldiers will be twenty miles long. Those who have horses must lead them. Some of the horses will slide on the ice and snow, and sometimes fall over the steep sides of the mountains. How can the cannon be carried over these passes?

The soldiers take large trees and hollow them out, and put the cannon into the hollow spaces in the trees. The horses can now draw the logs and cannon up the mountains.

VIEW OF HAVANA.

CUBA.

MORNING IN HAVANA.

What a beautiful view we have of the city of Havana from this bluff across the bay.

Do you think there are many hills in the city?

You can see the military hospital. Back of it stands the arsenal, with the American flag waving over it.

"Good morning, Castro, where are you going with your long line of horses?"

It is early morning. We are in Cuba, looking across the Harbor of Havana.

Castro is coming down the street with a dozen horses. He is riding on the first one. Each horse is tied by the nose to the tail of the horse in front of him.

"Your horses look very funny, Castro; where are they going?" "To take their bath, of course," answers Castro. "Down on the coral beach where the water is cool and shallow, we give a bath to all the cab horses and horses from the street cars every day." "Do they like it?" "Like it? Yes, indeed, for the sun is very hot in Cuba." "Is it ever cold here?" But Castro has gone into the shoals on his horse. Perhaps you can tell us about the seasons in Cuba.

MORRO CASTLE, HAVANA.

CUBA.

Across Havana Harbor you can see Morro Castle. It stands on a long point of land that reaches far out of Havana Harbor, like a protecting arm.

Morro is a great pile of stone. Inside the Castle are great guns, which can be aimed at any ship which is not wanted in the harbor.

Under the Castle is a deep dungeon. Prisoners do not

HAVANA HARBOR AND MORRO.

like to be sent there. High up on Morro Castle is the beacon light, which shows the sailor where to steer at night.

A short time ago no one was allowed to bring his vessel into the harbor at night. The vessels waited outside until sunrise, when they received a visit from the captain of the port; then, if every thing was satisfactory, they could enter the beautiful Harbor of Havana, and go up to one of its busy docks. Now the old rules are changed.

Let us take a walk. How narrow and crooked the streets are in Havana. Only the new streets are as broad as our own at home.

The walls of the houses are very thick. That is because they have earthquakes and hurricanes very often.

How bright the houses are. Some of them are painted white. This one is green, and the next one is dark blue.

Many of the houses are built of adobe. Where did we find other houses made of adobe?

The best houses are built much like those we find in Mexico. The rooms are built around a hollow square called a "patio." In the center there is a garden full of tropical plants, with a fountain, where people like to sit when it is hot. In the evening they can sit on the flat roof of the house, under the tall ferns that grow there in great tubs.

CHRISTOPHER COLUMBUS.

Do you remember the name of the first man who came across the Atlantic ocean? Cuba was one of the first islands which Christopher Columbus found. The Spaniards and some people of Havana believe that his body was placed in this cathedral.

Other people say that his son's body was brought here by mistake, and not Christopher's body. The

PATIO OF CUBAN HOME.

THE CATHEDRAL AT HAVANA.

church is built of coral rock, which looks like blocks of gray sponge.

The church is very old and not very clean on the outside. Inside there are many things which cost much money, but we like best to go and stand in the little corner where the body of the son of Columbus rested. They were both brave men.

A beautiful monument to Columbus was to be built in the middle of the church. The Spaniards have now taken the body back to Spain. Can you tell why they did this?

ON THE WHARVES.

"What do your people send away in those great casks and boxes, Castro?" "Haven't you heard of Havana

PLOWING IN CUBA.

cigars?" asks Castro. "I think you would find boxes and boxes of fine cigars in those cases."

Sure enough, and you send sugar from Cuba also, tied up in odd-looking bales. If you will look on the map you will see that Cuba is a long, narrow island. Nearly every one who lives here can reach the ocean very easily.

That is one reason why we have not more good roads.

People can take their fruit and sugar and tobacco to the coast and send it away on sailing vessels.

There are many towns along the coast where sailing vessels and small steamers come to buy fruit and sugar and tobacco.

What a clumsy yoke these oxen wear! The plow has only one handle, and is made of wood. Do you remember why the Mexicans would not use a steel plow?

CUBAN CARTMAN.

This wooden plow will not go down very deep, but the soil is so rich it is not necessary. Tobacco grows very well almost everywhere in Cuba.

We do not know what this man will plant, but we can be sure that whatever is planted will be ready to harvest in forty days. How many weeks in forty days? In how many weeks will corn ripen where you live?

One of our soldier boys planted some corn in front of his tent. In two days it was out of the ground. In five days it was ten inches high. Then came an order to break camp. The soldier pulled up his little corn stalk and sent it home in a letter. It had grown twelve inches in six days after it was a kernel of corn.

These carts are built to use in the narrow, crooked streets. The wheels are very large so that they may not be buried in the mud during the rainy season.

Very little wheel grease has been used on them, I am sure, for they creak badly as the poor oxen drag them slowly along.

What heavy yokes the oxen wear! Do you think four oxen would be needed to draw this cart over a good road? Did you ever see a farmer drive oxen? Did he walk beside them?

Can you guess what this farmer is bringing to market in his wagon? How do you think that he guides the oxen from his seat on the wagon?

TRAVELING FEED STORE.

What is this coming down the street? It looks like a row of four-footed hay-mows. Now we can see a horse's head coming out from each great load of hay. Sure enough, as they come nearer we find that each hay-mow has a horse under it.

Far away from the cities the roads are so poor that no cart can go over them. After every rainy season the farmer must take his machete with him to cut a path through the tangled thicket when he goes to market.

He makes a path wide enough for his pony and its load. The pony tramps patiently through the deep mud, as if he liked it.

Here is another four-footed market moving down the

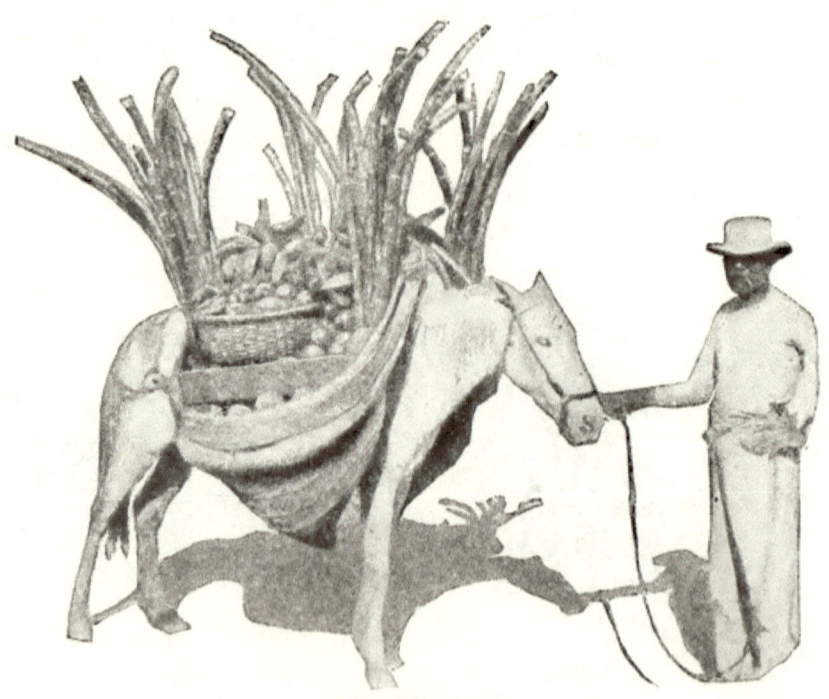

FOUR-FOOTED MARKET.

street to meet us. Can you see how many different things this market-man has loaded on the back of his patient pony?

Yes; there are mangoes and bananas, cocoanuts, pineapples, oranges, and lemons. Which will you buy?

The mangoes are reddish-yellow and speckled with black, and are about as large as a hen's egg. After you have eaten the pulp, which is yellow and very juicy, you will find a flat stone. Crack the stone, and you will like the meat inside.

HOW BANANAS GROW.

The Cuban children like bananas. Their mothers bake the green bananas in the oven. If you should prick the skin of a banana with a fork and bake it for twenty minutes, I think you would like it as well as they do.

If the banana could talk to you it might say, "I came from Cuba. While I was living near the top of our tall tree with its great, broad leaves, I saw a banana farm planted near us in the swampy woods.

"The trees were left standing to shade the men from the hot sun while they cut away the bushes and measured the farm with long ropes. Red tapes were tied six yards apart all along the rope.

"Men stretched the rope along the ground, and planted small shoots from banana trees at every red tape. Some carpets are a yard wide. Can you think how far apart the sprouts were set? The next week men came and cut down the forest trees. They left the sprouts to grow for six

BANANA ORCHARD.

months; then they came and cut down the grass and weeds near them with machetes. The sprouts grew very fast and were soon great trees."

At the end of a year big bunches of bananas could be cut from them. Will an apple tree bear good apples one year after it is planted?

There is a railroad track on this banana farm. The cars were sent down this track, and in two days all the great bunches of bananas were packed into them and sent to the New York boats waiting at the wharf.

The man who owned the farm received only thirty cents for a large bunch and fifteen cents for a smaller one. When the boat reaches New York the best bunches are sold for five dollars each.

We do not see many red bananas, because they do not keep as well on the long journey as the yellow ones. How many kinds of apples have you eaten? There are as many kinds of bananas as there are of apples. Many of the Cuban people build their houses of the Royal Palm or the banana tree.

THE MACHETE.

When Cuba belonged to Spain, the Cubans paid much of their money to the Spanish government in taxes. Some of the Cubans said, "We will govern ourselves, and be free from such heavy and unjust taxes."

The Spaniards said, "Send us money, or our soldiers will burn your homes and kill the men who do not obey us."

"Our children will starve if you take so much of our money," said the Cubans. "We will fight and save our homes. You have no right to make us obey you."

The Spanish soldiers were sent to Cuba with cannon and guns. The Cubans were ready to fight to save their homes, but they did not have enough money to buy guns. "If we cannot have guns, we will fight with our machete," said the brave Cubans.

The machete is a long steel blade with a bone handle. It was never made to fight with. The men had used it every day on their farms to cut down the tangled trees after a rain, or to beat down the bushes. They knew how

CUBAN CAVALRY ARMED WITH MACHETES.

to use the machetes very well. The Spaniards dreaded to see a little company of Cubans dash down upon them, even if they had no guns. They found that each Cuban knew how to swing a machete.

We are glad that the Cubans are free. They will never pay any more money to Spain. We hope there will never be another war where the machete will be used. The Cubans will be glad to use the machete only on their farms.

CUBAN VOLANTE.

THE VOLANTE.

What a strange carriage! Did you ever see one that looked at all like it?

What strange wheels, and what a queer top it has! This carriage is called a volante. Fifty years ago all the ladies in Cuba liked to drive about the cities in their volantes. Late in the afternoon or in the evening, when it became cool, the driver brought the volante to the door. The driver was dressed in a bright red suit trimmed with gold or silver lace and many buckles or bright buttons. The ladies liked to wear bright silk dresses, and fine lace shawls and scarfs.

The volantes looked very fine as they passed along the streets. Sometimes the lady in one volante would ask her driver to stop so that she might talk with a lady in another volante.

The ladies who did not care to drive walked up and down the broad walks near the city park or square. All were dressed very prettily and seemed happy.

The band played in the square every evening, and some of the boys and girls danced.

No one has seen a lady driving in a volante for many years now. There has been so much trouble in Cuba that the ladies have not cared so much about their pretty dresses.

When they ride now they go on horseback, or in carriages very much like those that you see every day. Many of the ladies who were rich and owned fine horses are very poor now.

OUR ROUGH RIDERS IN CUBA.

THE ROUGH RIDERS IN CUBA.

Have you heard of the Rough Riders in Cuba during the Spanish War? Col. Leonard Wood and Lieut.-Col. Theodore Roosevelt were the leaders. They gathered strong and hardy men from the east and the west, from the north and the south, from the cities and from the plains. These men were used to rough work and knew how to take care of themselves.

Many of them had been cowboys and could ride broncos, and could hit the mark every time with a rifle. They were brave men, and were glad when orders came for them to sail for Santiago.

Have you ever heard how they charged up San Juan Hill amid the rain of bullets from the Spaniards, who were hidden away in the blockhouse on top of the hill; how they, with other gallant soldiers, drove the Spaniards away and captured the forts, and finally captured Santiago?

When a Mauser bullet hits a man it knocks him down. As the men fell they did not scream or cry out. One man said quietly, "I'm hit!" Others said nothing. The wounded men knew that their friends who were fighting would be worried about them.

One of the fallen men said, "Let's sing a song to show our comrades that we are not dead." So while the bullets were flying about them, the brave fellows, some of whom were dying, sang the "Star Spangled Banner." After the war, General Wood became Military Governor of Santiago, and Colonel Roosevelt was elected Governor of New York.

TARANTULAS.

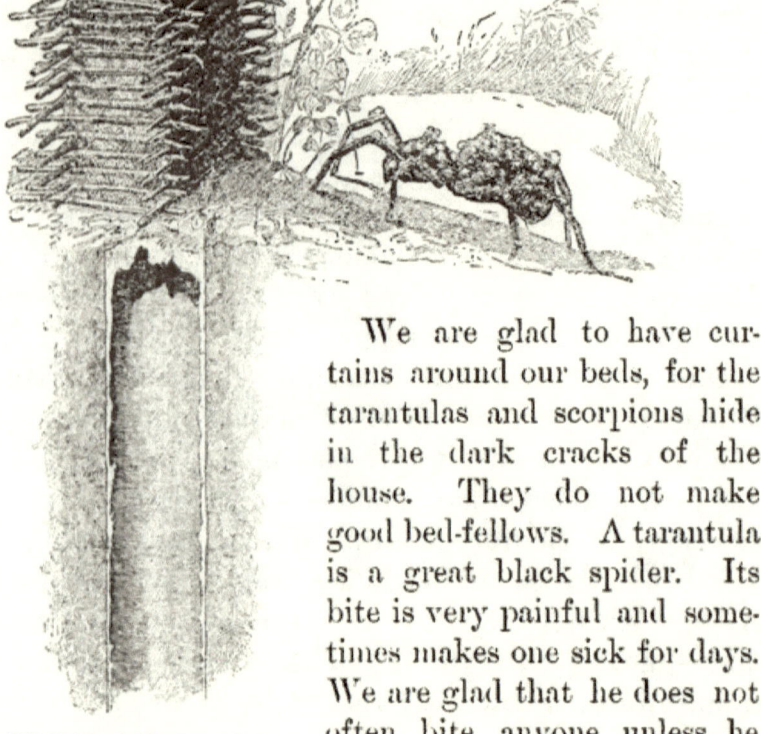

THE HOME OF THE TARANTULA.

We are glad to have curtains around our beds, for the tarantulas and scorpions hide in the dark cracks of the house. They do not make good bed-fellows. A tarantula is a great black spider. Its bite is very painful and sometimes makes one sick for days. We are glad that he does not often bite anyone unless he thinks he is in danger. You may go your own way, Mr. Tarantula; we do not care to play with you. The Tarantula often lives in holes in the ground, lining the sides with silk and covering the top with a tower of sticks, laid up as a woodman would build a log cabin, cementing it together with mud.

SCORPIONS

Scorpions look like tiny lobsters with long, pointed tails. At the tip end of the tail is a sting. Scorpions live on spiders and other insects. When the scorpion runs, it curls its tail up over its back; when it stings, it straightens the tail and brings it down suddenly. The wound swells and is very painful. The mother scorpion carries her baby about on her back, just as an Indian squaw carries her pappoose.

In Ceylon they grow to enormous size, some being twelve

SCORPION.

inches in length; but in Cuba they are only about four inches long. Sometimes they stow themselves away in a cargo of fruit, and then the men at Boston or New York, who are handling the fruit must be very careful, or Mr. Scorpion will make them remember him for many days.

A TROPICAL HOME.

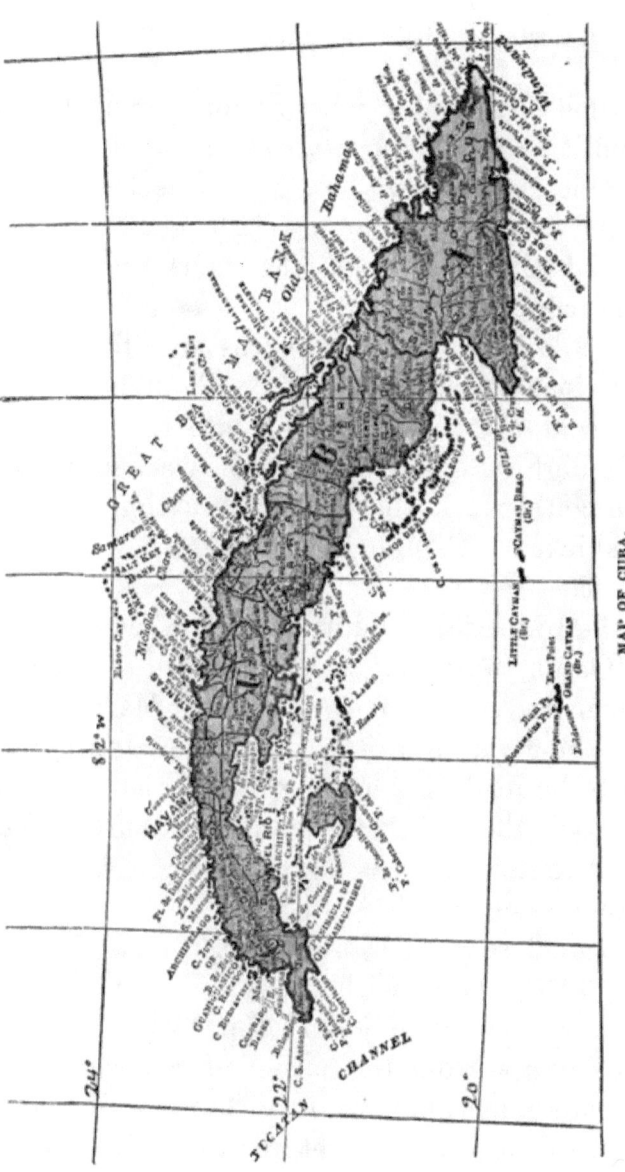

MAP OF CUBA.

THE BATTLESHIP "OREGON."

A short time before war with Spain began, this ship, which was built at San Francisco, was in Puget Sound.

Look on some map and see how far a vessel must sail to come by water from Puget Sound to Florida.

The name of this warship is the "Oregon." Captain Clark was her commander.

When the sailors knew that war was sure to come they were very anxious to take part in it. To make that long trip quickly coal must be shoveled into the furnace all day and all night. The engine-room was so very hot that no man could work there long at a time. But the men never shirked. Captain Clark said they begged to work overtime.

On went the beautiful warship, faster and faster, through the Pacific Ocean, until she came to Peru. There she stopped for more coal. The gunboat "Marietta" had been at Peru the week before, and had ordered hundreds of tons of coal to be ready for her big friend, the "Oregon."

Away around the southern point of South America came the "Oregon." It was a great voyage for a battle-ship to make at such speed.

The "Oregon" reached Florida in fifty-nine days, having steamed 14,700 miles without an accident. She only waited for more coal, then joined the fleet. When Cervera tried to escape from the harbor of Santiago on that beautiful Sunday morning of July 3d, one of the warships that helped destroy his fleet was the swift "Oregon."

BATTLESHIP "OREGON."

PORTO RICO.

A PORTO RICAN MILKMAN.

Moo! Moo! Listen; do you hear that call? It means "Good morning, won't you come and buy your milk for to-day?"

This milkman does not need any cans or bottles. He has no milk cart. If you bring out your pail he will milk into it. Then he will drive his cows down the street to the next house.

How many different ways of selling milk have you read about? Do you remember how the Mexican boys brought milk to town, and how the girls carried it in Switzerland, and in Norway?

It must be washing day at this woman's house. She is seated on a stone and has drawn the tub close to her. She never saw a clothes line. There are plenty of fresh green bushes back of her house. She will spread her clothes on the bushes to dry.

The working men and women like to wear coarse white clothes. They like to keep them clean, too.

Did you ever hear about the street-sweepers in a certain large city of America who wear white clothes and are called "White Wings"? Do you know who originated this custom?

PORTO RICAN LAUNDRY.

Have you seen men and women in your town dressed in white as they like to dress in Cuba and Porto Rico? This woman has spread many of her clothes on the grass to dry. You will not often see whiter clothes than those she has washed.

When she gets to market and unpacks her load she will cry, "Limes, lady, please buy my limes. You may have them for one dollar." The limes look like lemons, but a dollar is too much to pay, so we say, "No," and try to pass on. "Oh, but you may have them for half a dollar!"

GOING TO MARKET.

cries the market woman. "No, we do not care for them." "Then take them for a quarter of a dollar." We walk on again, and she runs after us, saying: "You may have them for ten cents." Does your market man change his prices like this?

We have eaten a great many kinds of fruits in Porto Rico that we never tasted before. We like the limes best of all. Limes are pickled and are sent to the United States. Did you ever eat a pickled lime?

Whoa, Victor; let us pick some of the fruit off this guava tree. It looks like little white pears, but it tastes more like spicy grapes.

We will peal off the smooth yellow rind and eat the

GATHERING GUAVAS.

pulp. The rind is thin and crisp. The seeds are spicy and sweet.

When I go home I will tell you about these guava trees, for you like guava jelly. I wish you could have some of the marmalade they make here from the rind.

There are many groves of guava trees in this part of Porto Rico. Now, go on, Victor, for we must get back to the fort before dark.

What a fine road! How firm and hard it is! It is made of crushed stone.

It is the only good road that we have found in Cuba or Porto Rico, and was made by the Spanish government. It is called the Military Road.

The men of Porto Rico were made to work on this road

A NATIVE'S HOME ON THE MILITARY ROAD.

at fifty cents a day. Spanish soldiers watched them while they worked, to see that they did not run away. They could find easier work and better pay on the farms. All along the road we find little forts in which the Spanish soldiers lived, and little houses where the natives live.

PORTO RICO.

No one could go over the road unless he had a letter from the Spanish government.

Good morning, Miguel; what game do you shoot in Porto Rico? "Oh, there are plenty of rabbits and ducks, and turkey and other game. We like to hunt in winter. Our winters are like the October weather in New England."

Sometimes we get up very early and go away off into the country. As soon as the sun rises the pigeons come to the mangleberry swamps by hundreds. While they are eating the mangle berries for breakfast we can shoot dozens of them.

These pigeons have queer little white top-knots on their heads. Their bodies are bluish black. My sister Melita likes to have me bring back enough pigeons for a big pigeon pie. She does not care for the rabbits and turkeys. This is a picture of Melita as she looked at a party last summer.

MIGUEL.

MELITA.

PEACE IN PORTO RICO.

A wonderful thing happened near Aybonito not long ago. Just beyond the town, at a place where the Military Road runs along the top of a high ridge, the Spanish

AYBONITO.

soldiers were waiting for the Americans. They were near a bend in the road and were hidden behind great rocks. Our men knew it would be like going into a trap to try

MAP OF PORTO RICO.

to pass the Spanish guns. But they must take the Military Road, so all were eager to go forward. They planted their cannon and formed their lines and were all ready to fire. The brave men stood waiting for General Brooke to order them to move forward.

Suddenly an officer came dashing through the ranks from the rear. He handed General Brooke a paper. It was a message with the news of peace. It came just in time to save the lives of many brave men, both Spanish and American. The battle would have been one of the most cruel of the war.

PHILIPPINES.

ALMOST four hundred years ago there lived a famous sea captain. What did he know about the earth? Very little indeed. But Magellan, this captain, wanted to know more. He wanted to show that the earth was round, by sailing around it.

MAGELLAN.

The king of Spain gave him five ships and more than two hundred men. Did he know where he was going? Not at all. Would we think now that we could cross the great ocean with a little sailing vessel? Many days and months and years he sailed. He came to South America, and to a great sea, which he called the Pacific Ocean.

At last he found the Philippine Islands. Can you guess why he gave them that name? He named them after King Philip, of Spain. Look on the map and you will see these islands.

Magellan landed on one of these islands, but he never left it, for he was killed by a chief. After three long years a single one of the five ships, with fifteen men, finally reached Spain.

A CARAVEL.

What had they done? They had proved that the earth was round. Can you show their journey on a map?

I am Mindacilla and I live on the island of Luzon. My skin is not white like yours. My eyes are black and

PHILIPPINE HOME.

my hair straight and long. My dress is white and is made of "pina" cloth.

My home is in a cocoanut grove. Our house is not on the ground, but is built on posts. In front of the house is the Pasig River. My father has many cocoanut trees.

We drink the milk in the nuts, and we eat the cocoanut meat.

Ropes are made from the fibre of this tree. The roof is

made out of the leaves. We should not know what to do without the cocoanut. I often go fishing with my father. I do not think you ever saw a fishing boat just like his.

Beside the boat there is a long raft. Do you see a long rope holding in place two tall poles? Of what is this long rope made?

By letting out this rope, the great net is lowered into

FISHING ON PASIG RIVER, MANILA.

the water. When my father is ready he draws up the rope, and raises the net. In the net we find fish; sometimes there are only a few, but often we catch a great many.

Little Mindacilla lives under the shadow of a high mountain. You would not want to, I am sure, when I tell you that it is the volcano Mayon.

You may well be afraid of it, for it is not a still volcano, but is one that is always in motion.

Mindacilla often watches the great column of black smoke that pours out of the top of the volcano. What happens when there is an eruption? Mindacilla does not mind the earthquakes that shake the ground. In the towns of this island the houses cannot be more than two stories high. Why?

Here is a picture of a church tower ruined by an earthquake. You would not care to be in a church during an earthquake.

WATCH TOWERS.

If you were to visit the Philippine Islands, you would see old stone towers near many villages. Why should there be so many, and what can they be used for? Most of the towers are old, and the rains and earthquakes have ruined some of them. Would you ever think of calling them watch towers?

RUINED CHURCH.

WATCH TOWER.

Yes; many years ago, day and night, men watched from the windows. They could see far out to sea, but what were they looking for? It was well they watched, for pirate ships sailed all around the coasts. What harm would the pirates do? Look at the picture and tell me.

These pirates would burn towns when they could. Many times they captured Spaniards and natives. They would kill the men and take the women and children away with them.

They made the women and little children their slaves. These pirates were good fighters.

In the picture you see something like a sword in the hand of this pirate. He would not call it by that name, but would tell you it is a "barong." He can cut very well with his "barong," for it is very sharp.

Why have these pirates given up

PHILIPPINE WARRIOR.

their visits? Perhaps you can tell when you know that the Spaniards have guns, and that the pirates had only "barongs," spears, and bows and arrows.

MORO CHIEFS, MINDANAO.

STREET IN NATIVE VILLAGE.

A NATIVE VILLAGE.

If you were to visit the island of Luzon, you would call it a great garden. Here is a picture of one of the towns. It has wide, smooth streets, which are so white that they glisten in the sunlight.

These streets are made of white coral, and are swept twice a day. What happens when there is a fire? Nothing is done to save the burning huts.

One afternoon three thousand of these houses were burned, and many people were left homeless. Sometimes some of the houses are pulled down to stop a fire from spreading. When there is a fire the people steal from one another. They often lose both their houses and their furniture. What kind of furniture do you think the Filipinos have in their houses?

You may think that these are summer houses. No; in one of these houses a little girl lives all the year round. One of Mindacilla's friends lives here and they often visit each other.

It is a pretty little hut, but oh, how small for a large family! Think how dark it must be inside. But there is the open door, and a window. In the place of glass is a thin oyster shell. What a small window!

In Mindacilla's house there are a number of windows. They are quite large, and have in them oyster shells, cut into squares. The squares are so small that there are *sometimes* two hundred in one window. The light from outside shines through the thin oyster shells.

MAP OF PHILIPPINE ISLANDS.

This boy is Sultan of the island of Sulu. What does that mean? Why, he is king of thousands of dark-colored people like himself.

Is he old enough to rule, now? No, it will be a number of years before he will be a real Sultan. Armies of men are ready to fight for him, yet he is always in fear of being killed.

I have seen another picture of the little Sultan. In that picture he was riding a beautiful black pony. Many of his soldiers were near him. One of them had on a suit of mail.

All of the soldiers had long swords, and some of them carried guns. If they were fighting, where would they carry their cartridges? If you should look at their cheeks you would see that they carried them in their mouths.

Many of their guns are very old, and with them these soldiers cannot hit a mark as our soldiers do.

SULTAN OF SULU.

Let us take a walk through the little town of Caloocan, near Manila. What shall we see? Early in the morning we shall find it cool and pleasant. All the business of the town is done between six and ten o'clock in the early part of the day. From ten o'clock until four o'clock you

PHILIPPINE ROAD HOUSE.

will see very few persons in the streets. Where is every one? It is so hot during the middle of the day that it is not safe to venture out, and all who can do so take their midday nap, called a "siesta," at this time. Late in the afternoon and in the evening every one comes out.

As we walk along the street shaded by the great palm

leaves, we see many little stores in front of the native houses, where refreshments are sold to the passerby. Here is a picture of a Philippine road house. Its roof and walls are made of matting and bamboo. You can buy all sorts of native refreshments here—bean porridge, fruit of all kind, and drinks, hot and cold.

WATER BUFFALO AND SLEDS.

It is very warm where Mindacilla lives. In her land there are the rainy and the dry seasons. How can Mindacilla's father get about out of doors in the rainy season?

MINDACILLA.

His water buffalo is the only animal that can carry him, and he rides "buffalo-back." He cannot go very fast in this way, in the deep mud and water. He is sure to come to a rushing stream, too deep for the buffalo to wade or swim through. The only way to travel now is by boat.

In the dry season Mindacilla often rides with her father on a buffalo sled. I think it must be hard for the buffalo, but he is very strong.

HAWAII.

Here we are at the Hawaiian Islands in the very middle of the great Pacific Ocean! We have come in a great steamer from San Francisco.

The water in the bay is as clear as crystal.

At the wharf we see many boys waiting to dive for the dimes which they hope will be thrown to them. Here is a dime; toss it toward the shore. Splash! go a dozen boys, and down they dive. One boy comes up with the dime, and holding it between his teeth turns a high somersault off the boards into the water. That is his way of saying "I thank you."

It is very funny, and while they are waiting to land, the people on the boat toss dimes to the boys. By the time we go ashore the quickest boys have their mouths full of dimes.

One day a small steamer called "Claudine" sailed away from Hawaii. The wharves were full of people to see her start. On board were five men whom they were sending to the United States Government at Washington. These men had been told to ask if Hawaii might become a part of the United States. After thinking about it five years, our government said "Yes." Now Hawaii is a part of our country.

STEAMER "CLAUDINE" LEAVING HONOLULU.

FLOWER GIRLS.

As we go up the street we find the flower girls sitting on their grass mats. Their flowers are made up into wreaths. Here come some girls to buy wreaths for their friends. The friends are going away on the boat, and the girls will toss the wreaths over their heads when they say good-by.

If there is a young man in the party they like to cover him with wreaths just to tease him.

Every one wears flowers. The wreaths are very beautiful. The flower girls try to find the finest flowers in the woods. They put them together so that the colors will look pretty. Sometimes they make a long rope of flowers.

Some of the flower sellers are Japanese girls. They are very happy in this country. Many of their people have come here to live.

LADIES ON HORSEBACK.

On holidays the ladies of Hawaii like to dress in this way when they ride horseback. They wear lovely wreaths of flowers, and put great wreaths around their horses' necks.

They do not use side-saddles, but wear a Pau instead. A Pau is a long, bright-colored cloth which is draped over the horse. It covers the stirrups and almost touches the ground. Here come ten women dashing down the street

HAWAIIAN LADY ON HORSEBACK.

on their horses. They ride so fast that the Paus fly straight out behind like bright-colored wings.

These people love horses, and almost every man and woman of the better class on the island owns at least one horse and can ride it well. The horses are very sure footed. They climb the mountains and creep along the narrow paths and do not fall. When Americans first came to this island there were no horses here. We are very glad that they brought horses and cows with them.

HOMES IN HAWAII.

You will not find many grass houses in Hawaii to-day. Long ago all the people lived in these houses. The frame of the house is made of bamboo poles tied together with ropes. The ropes are made of palm leaf fibers. The roof and the sides of the house are thatched with fine grass.

Do you know what "thatched" means? Nearly all the cooking and eating are done outside of the house. The people go inside the houses only at night or on rainy days. Think how Hawaii must have looked when all the houses were made of grass.

These people built their houses in much the same way as birds build theirs. A bird's little grass house is hung in the tree, so it needs a floor of grass and has no roof. These houses have no floor, for they are set on the ground. In a land where there are so many earthquakes such a house is safest. If your house should come tumbling down upon you, you would rather have it built of grass than of brick.

HAWAII. 213

When they made a grass house for their chief, the people braided ferns into the corners. The ferns turned black as the house grew older. The grass was straw-color when it dried. You could always tell a chief's house by the black corners.

Nearly all the people live in wooden houses now. Some

MODERN HOUSE IN HONOLULU.

of the people have built very handsome houses, with wide lawns in front and beautiful gardens back of them.

The poorer people like to build houses of wood that have open basements. They like to sleep on mats spread on the bare ground and to cook their food out of doors. Upstairs they always have a fine bedroom and a parlor. In the bedroom there are chairs, tables, a good straw carpet, and a bed made up as well as any you ever slept in. But these fine bedrooms and the parlor are for guests. The people who own the houses do not care to use them.

A WILD FLOWER.

Did you ever see a cactus called the Night-blooming Cereus? In Hawaii there are a great many of them. A wall around the college grounds in Honolulu is covered with these cacti.

NIGHT-BLOOMING CEREUS.

Some evening when it is time for the buds to open we will watch them. The buds tremble in the moonlight as if there was a little fairy inside making ready to come out. We watch closely, but the buds open so quickly and quietly that we are surprised every time. If a little fairy was in the flower she has slipped away on a moonbeam before we could see her. The flowers have large, soft, white petals. A sweet smell fills the air as they open. They are so beautiful we like to play that there really was a tiny fairy in each one. We like to think that a moonbeam coaxed her away to bathe in the dewdrops and play among the ferns and grasses. We can play that, when daylight comes, the merry sunbeams touch the little ladies from the flowers with magic wands and turn them all into butterflies.

THE SURF BOATS.

Each canoe is made out of one log. The men of Hawaii do not know how to steam their canoes and stretch them as the Alaskans do. The canoes are so narrow that they must have outriggers. An outrigger is a frame fastened to the side of a boat to help balance it.

All around the islands are rough coral reefs. Some day we will read about the coral. These reefs make the waves dash up so high that it is sometimes hard for small steamers to come to the wharfs. Then the men go out and bring the people to land in their little boats.

These men know just how to let the great waves catch their boats and take them toward the land. If you were watching you would think the little boats would be crushed by the great waves. But these men know how to manage boats in rough water. When the waves are highest these men like best to be on the water.

A LUAU OR PICNIC.

Will you come to our picnic?

In Hawaii we call it a "luau." You may help us get the feast ready if you like. Here are the mats made of grass. We will spread them on the ground. The men will hang larger grass mats up to make a tent, for the sun is very hot.

We will bring all the vines and ferns and flowers we can carry from the woods. The grass mat on the ground is our tablecloth. We will make table mats of ferns and put pretty vines all around the edge. Do you see how the men have trimmed the poles of our tent with vines? We love to have flowers around us.

Would you like to know what we shall eat at this feast? We shall have poi, roast pig, roast beef, sweet potatoes, shrimps, raw meat and fish, cocoanut pudding, watermelons, oranges, bananas, mangoes, alligator pears, and papaias. We may have fresh moss to eat with our salted kukui nuts.

Over there the men are making an oven in which the meat and fish will be roasted. We call the oven an "imu." They build a great fire in a deep hole and heat some stones very hot. When the wood has all burned away, the hot stones are taken out with a hoe.

Other people have been cutting up the meat and fish. They have put first the fresh taro and then the tough ki leaves around each bundle. Some wet banana leaves will be put over the fire in the imu. Then these bundles of meat will be put in. More wet banana leaves will be dropped in; then the very hot stones will be put over them. The stones will be covered with more leaves and the hole will be filled with dirt.

The heat in the stones will cook the meat; the wet leaves will steam and make it tender. The top leaves will keep the dirt from the bundles, and the dirt will keep the heat in the oven.

It is one o'clock in the afternoon now; at six o'clock our dinner will be cooked. A little bundle of meat and one of fish will be given to each person at the feast. You untie your bundle and eat the meat with your fingers. You will like the taro leaves, for they taste of the juice of the meat. You may not care to eat raw fish.

Perhaps you will not know how to eat poi and cocoanut pudding without a spoon. We dip it from the bowls and toss it into our mouths with the two first fingers of the right hand. No one ever has a spoon or a fork at a luau. But every one is glad to be here. We think it is the best kind of a picnic in the world.

A ROYAL FEATHER CLOAK.

Long ago the people of Hawaii believed many strange things. They thought that a king must have a royal cloak made of certain feathers. These feathers grew on a bird called the mamo.

Each bird had but two feathers of this kind—one under each wing. How many birds must have been caught before one of these cloaks could be made! Sometimes the mamo were set free after the two yellow feathers had been taken.

The little feathers were fastened into a strong piece of canvas. They made the canvas look as smooth and fine as yellow plush. This cloak was a yard and a half long and four yards wide at the bottom. You can see it in our museum when you come to Hawaii.

ROYAL CLOAK OF HAWAII.

The people thought, too, that a chief's bones made the best fishhooks. Some chiefs did not like to think that their bones would be made into fish-hooks after they were dead. One chief, called Pae, said, "I do not wish my bones made into arrows or into fish-hooks."

Two of his strong men said they would hide his body where no one could find it. After the chief was dead they wrapped him in his feather cloak and hid him in a deep cave. But some one found the bones and made a large hook of the thigh bone. They say the fish would come to this hook before it was baited. You can see the hook, too, in our museum.

PLANTING SUGAR CANE.

These men are planting sugar cane. Are their bags full of seed? No, they are planting pieces about a foot long cut from the cane near the top.

They will plant these cuttings in the ditches. The ditches run across a very wide field. They were made with a fine steam plow like those used on our very large farms. Americans own many of these sugar fields, and they use the very best plows or cultivators that they can buy.

After the cuttings are covered over with earth they will soon begin to grow. But the cane will not be ready to cut for a year and a half. Sugar cane grows wild in Hawaii.

The people once used the cane just as it grew. About sixty years ago a man made a large cane farm. He brought cuttings from the best cane in the world and planted them in his garden. He dug ditches across the farm and turned water into them, so that the cane need not be thirsty. He kept the weeds away.

Soon he had a very fine field of cane. He ground the cane in a mill and boiled out the sugar. When he sold the sugar, people said it was the best they had ever tasted. Next year the man had a larger farm and made much money. Since that time many people have planted sugar cane fields in Hawaii.

CUTTING THE SUGAR CANE.

The sugar cane is ripe. It looks like a field of tall corn. The long rows of silvery tassels wave on the tops of the cane. A hundred men will come to cut the cane. They must cut it very near the roots, for the part nearest the ground has the most sugar in it.

When it is all cut down it is taken to the mill. Every man who owns a large field of cane has a mill in which it can be ground. Men are sent to lay a railway on top of the ground. This railway is not fastened down. It is made so that it can be moved easily. One day it is put around one side of the field; the next day it is taken up and laid on the other side so that it can be used there. It is called a portable railway. Cars are run over this railway. They are filled with cane, and then run back over the railway to the mill.

The cane must be ground very soon after it is cut. The cars are run so fast that they sometimes run off the rails and tip over. Away go the great loads of stalks! But the men put the rails back, set the cars on them, fill them again, and go on as fast as ever.

The cars are drawn by a small steam engine. The owners ride about the fields on their horses to keep the

HARVESTING SUGAR CANE.

men at work, so that the cane will not spoil before it is ground.

Some of the men own only small fields and cannot afford to buy railways. They send their cane from the field to the mill on carts.

Sometimes the carts are drawn by horses. Sometimes the carts are very large and are drawn by eighteen or twenty young oxen. These young oxen are driven very fast by men who ride beside them on horseback.

If you meet two or three of these great carts coming down the road, you would better drive into some field and hold your horse until they have gone past.

The cane tops are cut off and left in the field. The roots are left in the ground. They will soon send up sprouts or suckers, from which next year's field of cane will grow.

RAISING TARO.

Did you taste of the poi at our picnic? Those of us who have always lived in Hawaii like poi better than anything else we have to eat.

Poi is made of a root. The root comes from a plant which grows in the water. It is called the taro plant. I think you have seen plants growing in ponds in America which look much like our taro.

Would you like to know how we help the taro to grow? First we make a bed of rich, soft mud in our garden. It need not be very large. Enough taro will grow on an acre of ground to last our family of eight all the year.

After we have made the garden bed we build a wall of earth all around it. Only one gate is left in the wall. In the soft mud we make hills, and in them plant pieces from the top of ripe taro root, very much as you plant potato eyes in potato hills.

After the roots are planted we let water run into the

BEATING THE TARO PLANT INTO FLOUR OR POI.

gate we left in the earth wall. The trenches must be kept full of water until the root is ripe—a whole year or more.

We like to plant taro at different times in the year, so that we may always have some fresh taro ready for use.

The taro yields us more food to a given space of land than any other crop, and it is very profitable.

We like the root boiled, baked, or fried, but we like it best when it is made into poi. If you boil the young leaves they taste like spinach.

MAKING POI.

We think we must have poi to eat every day. It is hard to make poi. We can have all the fruit and berries we wish without much labor. We can swim out on the waves and catch fish in our hands, but we like poi to eat with them.

The men always made it, but now they often hire the Chinese to do it for them. A Chinaman will work all day for very little money.

If we make our poi ourselves, we bake the roots first and then scrape them. Then we make a paste.

The paste is set away to rise over night; then we mix enough water with it to make a porridge, and our poi is ready for use.

No one is made sick by eating poi. In one of our cities there is a large mill where taro flour is made. This flour is sold to the people of the United States. They make it into cakes, and muffins, and puddings. It is very good for sick people.

Some day more people in the United States may buy our taro flour. Our people have lived on poi for hundreds of years.

RICE FIELDS.

Many Chinese have come to Hawaii to live. Do you know what food the Chinese like best? Yes, it is rice. Men who own rice fields always hire Chinamen to work in them. Nearly all the work in a rice field must be done by men standing in the water. Only Chinamen are willing to do this.

One small field is sown with rice seed, and the water is allowed to run over it. When the plants are six

RICE FIELD, HAWAII.

inches high the water is let out. The little plants are then pulled up and planted a few inches apart in the large field.

The little plants are tied up in great bales. The Chinamen carry the bales on their backs and plant the sprouts in the mud under the water, in the larger fields.

After the rice is well started, fresh water must be

turned into the fields every day. The water comes from the hills in ditches which must be dug for it.

Rice will ripen in six months. After the little kernels begin to grow, so many small birds come to eat them that they would all be destroyed if the Chinamen did not frighten them away. It is very funny to see them wading up and down the rice swamps in their queer round hats, beating drums, firing crackers, and shooting at the little bird robbers.

When the rice is grown, the water is turned off, and the rice-straw left for a little while to ripen in the sun. Then the Chinamen come and cut the rice with sickles.

After it has dried in the sun for a day it is tied up in bundles. A bundle is hung on each end of a stick. Each stick is lifted to the shoulder of a Chinaman. Then twenty or thirty of them go in a long line at a sort of dog-trot to the threshing floor, which may be half a mile away.

Chinamen like to do all the work on a rice field in their own way. They do not care for carts or railways to help them carry home their rice.

They do much of their work in the hardest way, but they raise very good rice. Thousands of dollars' worth of rice are sent from Hawaii to the United States every year, and the Chinamen raise nearly all of it.

www.ingramcontent.com/pod-product-compliance
Lightning Source LLC
Chambersburg PA
CBHW021841230426

43669CB00008B/1040